Cooking with Loula

Cooking with Loula

Greek Recipes from My Family to Yours

ALEXANDRA STRATOU

ARTISAN
NEW YORK

And then the day came,
when the risk to remain tight
in a bud was more painful
than the risk it took to blossom.

—Anaïs Nin

Library of Congress Cataloging-in-Publication Data

Names: Stratou, Alexandra
Title: Cooking with Loula / Alexandra Stratou.
Description: New York : Artisan, [2015] | Includes index.
Identifiers: LCCN 2015037679 | ISBN 9781579656683
Subjects: LCSH: Cooking, Greek. | Stratou, Alexandra—Family. | LCGFT:
Cookbooks.
Classification: LCC TX723.5.G8 S77 2015 | DDC 641.59495—dc23 LC record available at
http://lccn.loc.gov/2015037679

Photographs by Ioanna Roufopoulou
Design by Toni Tajima

Artisan books are available at special discounts when purchased in bulk for premiums and
sales promotions as well as for fund-raising or educational use. Special editions or book
excerpts also can be created to specification. For details, contact the Special Sales Director at
the address below, or send an e-mail to specialmarkets@workman.com.

Published by Artisan
A division of Workman Publishing Company, Inc.
225 Varick Street
New York, NY 10014-4381
artisanbooks.com

Published simultaneously in Canada by Thomas Allen & Son, Limited.
Printed in China
First printing, April 2016

10 9 8 7 6 5 4 3 2 1

To Kyria Loula,
who cooked the food I ate growing up,
and Giagia Sofia,
who taught me the importance of family.

Contents

There Is a Land

There is a land.
One land, governed by invisible laws.
Laws written in the wrinkles of the people.
In the tales told, untold, by mouths in whispers within walls of territory
known, unknown.
Fleeting free moment, where that one land appears just as it is to eyes
awaiting to be.
The words, the lives, the food that form a bridge that can be walked upon
and tasted.

I travel back and forth to past and present time.
To a future that is mine to make, with eyes that saw that one that is.

She visited her own then, with me today.
She crossed those lines as I do now.
We went there holding hands into that past unknown to me.

They were then aristocratic, she was poor.
Grand as they were, they feasted and they who served them filled their empty
insides as they could with what was left.
Lovingly she does recall, not bitter like today, when the middle has been found
and lost to a new divide of aristocratic poor.
I am convinced with every passing day that this divide no longer shall endure.
The time has come for one land to be one, not to my eyes but to all eyes
and somehow, unknown to me today, there shall be food for all.

Foreword

GREECE, the cradle of Western civilization, taught mankind many of the most important principles of life—among them was the value of cooking and sharing food with others.

When Alexandra told me of her intention to create a book based on her experiences of family and food, I understood that she would be honoring the rituals with which she was raised and capturing the legacy of her beloved teacher, Kyria Loula.

This is not a typical Greek cookbook, like those tourists buy to remember the meals they had by the sea. This book allows us to enter the kitchen of a Greek family that enjoys sharing, revealing their cherished annual traditions, and their ingredients, and their life cycles. It inspires us to cook and, above all, to share.

As I hold this book in my hands, the image of a relay race comes to mind in which one passes a baton to the next receptive hand. In a similar fashion, the family seed, a farmer's most precious inheritance, is handed down from generation to generation.

The task of gathering the knowledge of our ancestors is respectful and insightful; transmitting it—riddled with stories—is an act of generosity that contributes to the preservation of cultural diversity. Cultures of people, rooted to the land where they are born and from which they obtain their precious produce. Food artisans, who, each season—to the delight of cooks, foodies, and apprentice kitchen magicians alike—fill the markets with their produce.

Why does food become a channel for memory? Food made well and shared is an act of surrender, care, and love, while at the same time a celebration of color, rhythm, community, excitement, happiness, and pleasure. Who does not want to be part of this celebration?

Generations unite over steaming pots, hands work skillfully with decisiveness, and all is flooded with marvelous aromas. These same aromas, gestures, and traditions transport us, time and time again, to that uniquely magical moment of creation and offering. Sharing this legacy with others is a gift, one for which I shall always be grateful.

—VISI IRIZAR, director of the
Luis Irizar Cooking School,
San Sebastián, Spain

Introduction

MOST OF THE TIME, cooks wait until they become renowned before they decide to write a cookbook, and everyone waits in anticipation until they can buy the book to make all their delicious recipes. I am starting the other way around. I went to the Luis Irizar Cooking School in San Sebastián, Spain, and, a few years later, I bring this cookbook to life.

Cooking with Loula is a result of my love of food, but also my love of words; food is the means I use to bring people together, and words are what I use to express the things that I see in life as enchanting. In this book you will find a collection of my family's Greek recipes, surrounded by my ideas on food. Everything is presented through my lens and with my aesthetic, both of which have been heavily influenced by what I have been exposed to growing up.

The idea for this endeavor was born after spending time with my eldest cousin, Alexia, and her then one-year-old daughter, Nefeli. It occurred to me that with our family cook, Kyria Loula, getting too old to cook for us, our working mothers with little time on their hands, and the older members of our family, who connect us to our roots, dwindling, there would be no way to share the tastes of our childhood with the newest addition. I felt the urge to collect these significant pieces of our past and pass them on to various family members to share with their own families, in the hope that these pieces could contribute to the building of their own sense of belonging, just as they have contributed to mine.

The process of collecting recipes began with weekly visits to Kyria Loula's home, where she offered not only recipes, but also direct access to my family's world from an outsider's perspective. Kyria Loula—*Kyria* meaning "Mrs." in Greek—started working at my great-grandmother's house at a very young age, and then cooked for different members of my family on a weekly basis. She passed away while I was writing this book, so my great-aunt filled in the majority of the missing recipes, while the people who had worked with Kyria Loula in the kitchens of our homes contributed details that I could not have otherwise recovered. My great-uncle, who in my eyes embodies that which I call family, talked and still talks to me about my family in general, about the people I never met, and the things that happened before my birth. My first cousins brought some of the recipes in this book to life by sharing their food-related memories. Giagia Sofia, my grandmother, who will never know about this book, is responsible for creating a lot of my family memories. She is the person who gathered us, without exception, on Sundays for family lunch, and the one who overcame the differences and difficulties that families are often characterized by in a way I admire. My parents upheld our family's food rituals and made sure that I participated in them actively. As a result, the recipes, stories, and sentiments in this book are the product of a combined effort made by various important people in my life.

As a Greek who has had many foreign influences throughout my life—I went to a very British school in Greece, had a Scottish nanny, and studied in the United States and Spain—I discovered in the writing of this book that it is food that has created a cultural home within me and has been the source of identity I always thought I lacked. I came to realize that it is vital to integrate the past you have known with the person you are today and the person you wish to be tomorrow. This is a process that entails looking at what you have lived, seeing your experiences exactly as they are, and choosing whether you want to move beyond them, leave them right where they are, keep them close, or put them in a special place for future reference.

Apart from being a personal food memoir, this book is meant to encourage you to relate to one another through something as basic as a meal and the memories thereof. The recipes you will find here are tried and tested. They have passed through the kitchens of three generations and are still revered. They are the foods that shaped my palate and have taught me what I like and do not like. They are healthy and homey and traditional, but not without refinement.

In order to write this cookbook I asked many questions, heard many stories, thought for hours about food, and consulted people inside my family and out. In doing so, I came to the conclusion that this cookbook is as much about my family as any other. We all have our own stories, our own tastes, our own memories, but no matter what they are, when talking about them we speak the same language. The places of the past we travel to are highly personal, but the journey is universal.

As a core element of who we are, food is a great place to start on this journey of self-exploration, and as this cookbook has proven an invaluable companion in forging my own path, I can only wish for it to have the same impact on yours.

I welcome you to my world and the atmosphere of remembrance that I have tried to create. I hope you hold this book in your hands and take some time—not only to cook, but also to contemplate, and to think, not about my past and what it means to me, but rather about your past and what it means to you. *Cooking with Loula* is about cooking, but ultimately, it is about what happens when people come together to eat the food that has been cooked. It is about the conversations that take place and the feelings that arise in the sharing of a meal without pretention. *Cooking with Loula* is an offering to others.

A Place to Start

COOKING is intricately connected to time; it is about the total time you need to go from start to finish, but also what you do with the time that's in between. It is about how you interact with what you cook, how much you listen to yourself as you are working, how present you are, and how much attention you give to the process.

Often during my recipe-collecting sessions with Kyria Loula, she skipped over valuable details that had become so ingrained in her over the years that she didn't think it was necessary to mention them. One of my challenges was to extract all of these little secrets, and my favorite part of the process was getting her to share what she heard the food tell her. After years of cooking and observing food as it cooks, she knew when a stew was asking for more water, or the onions were crying out to be drowned in wine, or the ground meat had had enough of being stuck to the bottom of the frying pan and was ready for tomatoes and water.

When writing each of the recipes, I wanted to communicate all of these small but important details, without overelaborating and scaring you away with huge amounts of text. So in the next few pages, you will find a distillation of her most important advice, along with some contributions of mine—things that I have picked up in my few years of experience that I think will make all the difference to your cooking.

Pantry Staples

In order to make the dishes in this book everyday options, your pantry needs to be stocked with some basic ingredients that often appear in these recipes.

Extra-virgin olive oil

Sea salt

Black peppercorns

Allspice berries

Bay leaves

Dried oregano

Garlic

Ground cinnamon

Juniper berries

Canned diced tomatoes

Tomato paste

Potatoes

Red or white onions

Pasta

Bread or crackers

Breadcrumbs

All-purpose flour

Granulated and powdered sugar

Honey

Large farm-fresh eggs

Greek yogurt

A young yellow cheese, such as a mild Graviera or Gruyère

Stock, homemade (see pages 209–212) or store-bought

Frame of Mind

Just as important as the ingredients you use is the frame of mind you adopt when you go out to buy them. Try to adhere to these guidelines, as they will bring you closer to the experience of eating and cooking in Greece.

- Get to know your local farmers and producers so that you can source quality ingredients and support local initiatives.

- Stand by your personal preferences. Do not choose convenience over quality.

- Make sustainable and ethical decisions when choosing ingredients.

- Use your senses—touch, sight, and smell—in order to select the best meat, fish, and produce.

- Find out what vegetables are available locally and in what months of the year, and use out-of-season ingredients only in moderation.

- When buying imported Mediterranean ingredients, buy them when they are in season in the Mediterranean. (See "Cooking with the Seasons," pages 28–29.)

- Try to find local alternatives to the suggested Greek products, or find small Greek producers exporting quality produce.

Cooking Tips

Cooking is much more than just knowing how to follow a recipe. It's a process; it is about starting a conversation with food, developing a language with the ingredients, and watching and learning how they interact.

- Prepare the scene. Start by setting out your ingredients.

- Add a little salt at the beginning of the cooking process and salt your food to taste at the end.

- Whenever you use tomatoes, let your mixture boil vigorously until nearly all liquid evaporates.

- Add some sugar if your sauce ends up tasting too acidic.

- Use your stovetop's smallest burner when making a stew.

- Meat goes through two phases when stewed: hard and then soft. Give it time to go through this cycle.

- Never add all of the water to a recipe at once; do so little by little.

- Do not use too much olive oil when you cook; drizzle as much as you like on the cooked dish before serving.

- Use freshly ground black pepper unless otherwise specified.

- When adding alcohol to a recipe, boil it until you can't perceive the alcohol when you inhale the vapor at a safe distance from the pot. Inhale at various times as it boils.

- Do not cook in a hurry!

- To sauté or brown: Place your pan on the heat, add a thin layer of oil, heat the oil, and then add the ingredient you want to sauté.

- Replace store-bought products with their homemade counterparts, whenever you have the time to make them.

- Bless your food when you reach the point where it could turn into a success or a failure.

Note: Both U.S. and metric measurements have been provided throughout the book, and have in some cases been rounded off for ease of use.

Essential Tools

Here is the complete list of tools (minus the electrical appliances) that I used to cook and test each recipe in this book. I include it here because even if this is by definition a Greek cookbook, I also consider it a starting point from which you can learn basic cooking techniques, begin to experiment with your own tastes, and build your own traditions. The first step in this process is to equip your kitchen with the essential tools you'll need.

1. Baking pans
2. Frying pans
3. Glass baking dish
4. Grater
5. Large chef's knife
6. Large saucepan or stockpot with lid
7. Loaf pan
8. Measuring cup
9. Mixing bowls

Cooking with the Seasons

A Mediterranean Fruit and Vegetable Guide

Spring

Almonds

Amaranth Greens

Artichoke

Butterhead Lettuce

Dandelion

Fennel Bulbs

Garlic

Green Peas

Lemons

Mandarin Oranges

Mint

Olives

Onions

Oranges

Parsley

Pistachios

Potatoes

Romaine Lettuce

Rosemary

Scallions

Spinach

Strawberries

Walnuts

Summer

Almonds

Amaranth Greens

Apples

Apricots

Basil

Beet Greens

Beets

Celery

Cherries

Cucumbers

Damson Plums

Dill

Eggplants

Figs

Garlic

Grapes

Green Beans

Green Bell Peppers

Green Peas

Lemons

Melon

Mint

Nectarines

Olives

Onions

Parsley

Peaches

Pears

Pistachios

Plums

Potatoes

Red Bell Peppers

Rosemary

Strawberries

Tomatoes

Walnuts

Watermelon

Zucchini

Fall

Almonds
Amaranth Greens
Apples
Basil
Beet Greens
Beets
Broccoli
Butterhead Lettuce
Carrots
Cauliflower
Celeriac
Celery
Chestnuts
Damson Plums
Dill
Fennel Bulbs
Garlic

Grapefruit
Grapes
Green Beans
Green Cabbage
Leeks
Lemons
Mandarin Oranges
Mint
Olives
Onions
Oranges
Parsley
Pears
Pistachios
Pomegranates
Potatoes
Red Cabbage

Romaine Lettuce
Rosemary
Scallions
Spinach
Tomatoes
Walnuts
Winter Squash

Winter

Almonds
Apples
Beets
Broccoli
Carrots
Cauliflower
Celeriac
Celery
Chestnuts
Fennel Bulbs
Garlic
Grapefruit
Green Cabbage

Leeks
Lemons
Mandarin Oranges
Olives
Onions
Oranges
Pistachios
Potatoes
Red Cabbage
Spinach
Walnuts
Winter Squash

Weekdays

Eating well on a weekday is about planning. With limited time on our hands during the workweek, it is easy to default to ordering in or cooking up dishes that require no time at all to make. Once in a while, this way of eating can be gratifying, though I believe that it cannot build a taste of home. The recipes in this chapter thus vary in complication. Some dishes are so simple they are easily made in under half an hour on days you just do not feel like cooking; others are more elaborate.

Weeknight dinners in my house were spent at the table with my older brother and my parents. These were moments where we coexisted just as we were: tired, happy, sad, talkative, or silent. The dinners we ate were cooked on Mondays by Kyria Loula, stored in the freezer, and later defrosted. I remember my mother talking on the phone every Sunday night with Kyria Loula, figuring out the food for the upcoming week. My mother was very adamant that we have a balanced diet, and together they tried to keep things interesting.

Weekdays are about ingredients that speak for themselves and offer nutrition to our body and soul. Unlike a weekend meal, a weekday meal is most definitely not a feast, but contributes substantially to our basic subsistence. In my eyes, weekday meals are daily moments of repose, where we can take in what was lost during the day, literally and metaphorically.

Soutzoukakia

SPICED MEATBALLS IN TOMATO SAUCE

This is one of the first traditional meals I made away from home, while in my senior year at college. I wanted to share the flavor with my roommate, so I called home to get the recipe. I find that when someone tells you a recipe, they tell you a story. You feel the atmosphere around the cook who makes it, and this atmosphere, when carried into your kitchen, is the ingredient that will make all the difference to the taste.   serves • 8 to 10   time • Under 2 hours

1 small potato, peeled and
  cut into 1-inch pieces

1 large onion, peeled and cut into
  1-inch pieces

3 cloves garlic

2 slices stale bread, crusts
  removed and slices soaked
  in water

1²/₃ pounds (750 grams)
  ground beef

1 large egg

2 tablespoons white wine vinegar

2 teaspoons ground cumin

Salt and pepper

All-purpose flour, for dredging

Extra-virgin olive oil

1 large eggplant, finely diced

½ cup (140 grams) tomato paste

1 teaspoon sugar

¾ cup (180 milliliters) red wine

1 cup (250 milliliters) Chicken
  Stock (page 211)

Purée the raw potato, onion, and garlic in a food processor, and add a little water. Transfer to a large mixing bowl. Squeeze excess water from the bread and add to the bowl along with the beef, egg, vinegar, 1 teaspoon cumin, salt, pepper, and a drizzle of olive oil. Knead with your hands. Add more cumin, salt, and pepper to taste. (You may brown a small ball of the beef mixture in a frying pan first if you prefer not to taste it raw.)

Lay a large piece of foil on your work surface and dust with flour. Take a full teaspoon of the beef mixture and roll it into an oval shape—it should be small and delicate, about the size of a cherry tomato (1½ inches / 4 centimeters) in length. Dredge in flour.

Heat a large frying pan over medium high heat and add a ½-inch (1-centimeter) layer of olive oil. Add the meatballs to the hot oil and brown on all sides, working in batches. Remove from the pan and position neatly in a baking dish.

Preheat the oven to 350°F (180°C).

Discard the used oil in the frying pan and add fresh oil. Heat over medium high heat. Add the eggplant to the hot oil and cook until softened. Remove from the pan and transfer to a plate. Discard the oil and wipe the pan clean with a paper towel.

Add a generous drizzle of oil to the cleaned frying pan, then add the tomato paste, remaining teaspoon of cumin, sugar, salt, and pepper. Bring to a boil, then add the wine and let the alcohol evaporate (see page 25). Add the stock and boil for 10 minutes, until reduced by half. Add the eggplant, stir well, bring to a boil, and then remove from the heat. Pour the sauce over the soutzoukakia in the baking dish.

Bake in the oven for 45 minutes, adding water every so often if the sauce gets dry.

tip

Make this dish without the eggplant when it is out of season.

Spanakopita

SPINACH PIE

To make a pie, one simply has to contain ingredients inside layers of dough. I imagine that at some point there were no recipes for them, as they were just filled with leftovers or abundant produce from a family's vegetable garden. Pies are perfect when you need to feed large groups of people—you can make them in advance, they don't need much fussing over, and people always love them! This spanakopita recipe has earned me many moments of glory, and I hope it will do the same for you.   serves • 6 to 8   time • Under 2 hours

Extra-virgin olive oil

1 medium onion, finely chopped

1 large leek, finely chopped

1 pound (500 grams) various greens, such as chard, washed, stems removed, and leaves coarsely chopped

1 pound (500 grams) spinach, washed, stems removed, and leaves coarsely chopped

18 ounces (500 grams) crumbled feta cheese

3 large eggs

Pepper

One 8-ounce (225-gram) package phyllo dough

Coat a large frying pan with olive oil and place over medium high heat. Add the onion and leek and cook until golden. Add the greens and spinach, cover the pan with a lid, and allow to wilt. Add a bit of water if the pan becomes too dry. Remove from the heat and drain to remove any excess liquid before transferring the greens to a bowl. Mix in the feta, eggs, and pepper. Taste and season, if needed.

Preheat the oven to 350°F (180°C).

Brush a 13-by-9-inch (33-by-23-centimeter) baking dish or baking pan with olive oil. Start the pie by laying a phyllo sheet on all four sides of the baking dish. Each sheet should partially cover the bottom of the dish, with the rest hanging over the edge. Brush every piece of phyllo that you lay on the dish with oil. Then place five sheets in the center, brushing each with oil. Add the filling and spread it out evenly.

Place five more sheets of phyllo over the filling, brushing each with oil, then fold over the overhanging sheets that you started with. Cut any excess phyllo away with scissors or a knife and use your pastry brush to tuck the phyllo in around the edges of the dish. Score the top with a sharp knife, marking the pieces you wish to cut later. Sprinkle with a little water.

Bake in the oven for 45 minutes to 1 hour, until the phyllo is golden brown.

Gemista

STUFFED TOMATOES AND PEPPERS

The history of my relationship with food can be separated into before and after cooking school. Before cooking school, I never read recipes, I loved food, and I loved sharing meals. I used my taste memory to get the results I wanted and only called home for help if I couldn't taste my way through something. After cooking school, there was a right and wrong way to approach cooking. There was a process, an order, and specific recipes, and I acquired a sort of absurd attitude that led me to cook things without really listening to or feeling what was going on with the food I had in front of me. I ended up believing that I didn't really need anyone or anything to show me what needed to be done—I was suddenly all knowing. But when I tried to make stuffed tomatoes, twice, I failed grandly! Testing the recipe for this book and seeing that, when I followed my family's age-old recipe, I could make fantastic stuffed tomatoes, I was reassured. The weight of having to succeed at everything alone, just because I had become a chef, was lifted off my shoulders. I was now accompanied by the past generations of my family.   serves · 8 to 10   time · Under 2 hours

6 medium tomatoes

6 green bell peppers

1½ cups (350 milliliters) extra-virgin olive oil

2 onions, grated

2 cloves garlic, crushed

¾ cup (150 grams) uncooked short-grain rice

⅔ cup (80 grams) pine nuts, toasted

Handful each of dark and golden raisins (about ½ cup / 40 grams total)

½ cup finely chopped parsley leaves (about ½ bunch)

1½ tablespoons dried mint

Sugar, as needed

Salt and pepper

6 tablespoons breadcrumbs

1 tablespoon tomato paste

Cut a small cap off the tops of the tomatoes and bell peppers and reserve. Remove the seeds and white pith from the insides of the bell peppers and discard. Scoop out the insides of the tomatoes using a spoon, working over a bowl to catch all of the pulp. Place the hollow bell peppers and tomatoes in a baking dish, ensuring they fit snugly. Purée the tomato pulp in a blender or food processor until smooth.

Add about 6 tablespoons of the olive oil to a large frying pan over medium heat. Add the onions and the garlic and cook until soft and translucent. Add the puréed tomato, increase the heat, and bring to a boil. Reduce the heat to a simmer and cook until the sauce has thickened and little liquid remains. Reserve 2 tablespoons of tomato sauce in a small bowl for later. With the frying pan still on the heat, add the rice, pine nuts, and raisins and stir to coat with tomato sauce. Cook the mixture for 8 minutes, stirring it every so often to make sure it doesn't stick to the bottom of the pan. Take the frying pan off the heat and add the parsley, mint, 1 teaspoon sugar, salt, and pepper. Stir well.

Preheat the oven to 350°F (180°C).

Season the inside of each vegetable with salt, pepper, and a pinch of sugar. Fill each with the rice mixture until three-quarters full, using about 1½ tablespoons of filling. Add 1 tablespoon of olive oil to each, then cover with their reserved caps. Brush the outsides of the vegetables with olive oil, and sprinkle them with breadcrumbs. Add enough water to the baking dish to reach one-quarter of the height of the vegetables, and add the reserved tomato sauce and the tomato paste to the water.

Bake in the oven for a little over an hour, or until the tomatoes and bell peppers are wrinkly like raisins. Add water while baking if the dish goes dry.

In Greece, dishes like this one are called ladera, *which means "stewed in oil"; this is why the quantity of olive oil called for in this recipe is much more than what I would regularly use.*

Pastitsio

Many adults secretly dream of being a child again—not in age, but in attitude. There is a yearning for those days of careless existence, when time is slow and things miraculously happen just the way they should. Each one of those adults pays tribute to this inner child through various means; eating foods that evoke memories of childhood is one of them. This recipe is a personal favorite of my cousin Sofia; knowing her, it seems natural that she would love this dish—the simplicity, the unpretentious taste, the texture, all bring back that unforgettable feeling of an uncomplicated life.   serves · 6 to 8   time · Under 3 hours

1 recipe Kimas (page 217)

One 16-ounce (500-gram) package bucatini or penne pasta

Olive oil

1 recipe Béchamel (page 216)

½ cup (50 grams) grated Kefalotiri or Parmesan cheese

½ cup (50 grams) grated Graviera or Gruyère cheese

Prepare the kimas as instructed on page 217. Meanwhile, cook the pasta. Bring a large pot of salted water to a boil over high heat. Once boiling, add the pasta and boil until al dente (tender but firm to the bite). Drain the pasta and drizzle with some olive oil. Set aside.

Prepare the béchamel as instructed on page 216. Once ready, remove from the heat.

Preheat the oven to 350°F (180°C).

Lightly grease a 13-by-9-inch (33-by-23-centimeter) baking dish with olive oil. Spread a thin layer of béchamel over the bottom of the dish. Begin layering with a third of the pasta, a sprinkling of the cheeses, and a few spoonfuls of béchamel. Top the pasta with half of the kimas and another sprinkling of the cheeses. Repeat the layers, ending with the pasta. Finally, pour half of the remaining béchamel over the top of the dish, then stick a fork between the layers of the pastitsio, and move it around to distribute the béchamel evenly. Top with the last of the béchamel, and then the remaining cheese.

Bake in the oven for 45 minutes, until the top is golden brown. Cool for 15 minutes before slicing and serving.

Kokkinisto Kotopoulo

TOMATO-STEWED CHICKEN WITH ORZO

I used to hate close-ended questions, because I never wanted to be tied down to one answer—but once I became a professional chef, I only got close-ended questions. Favorite dish? Most impressive recipe you make? Ultimate comfort food? I learned pretty fast that I could answer according to my mood. The only answer I never really changed was about comfort food. My ultimate comfort foods are simple dishes that elicit emotion in me. This recipe is one such dish. Though very simple, it has a basic goodness that nourishes my soul.

serves • 4 to 6   time • Under 2 hours

1 whole free-range chicken, about 4 pounds (2 kilograms), cut in pieces

Salt and pepper

2 whole cloves

1 large onion, peeled and left whole

Extra-virgin olive oil

½ cup (125 milliliters) red wine

6 medium tomatoes, grated, or one 14-ounce (400-gram) can diced tomatoes

2 juniper berries

2 allspice berries

3 cups (500 grams) orzo

1 tablespoon unsalted butter

Season the chicken with salt and pepper. Stick the cloves into the onion.

Cover the bottom of a large pot with olive oil and place over high heat. Add the chicken and onion. Brown the chicken on all sides. Add the wine and boil until the alcohol has evaporated.

Add the tomatoes, juniper, allspice, and a pinch of salt. Add water to barely cover the chicken; then cover with a lid. Bring to a boil, then reduce to a simmer and cook for about 1 hour.

Meanwhile, put a large pot of salted water over high heat and bring to a boil. Add the orzo and boil for 8 minutes. Drain well and set aside.

Preheat the oven to 350°F (180°C).

Using tongs, transfer the chicken to a deep ceramic baking dish. Discard the onion. Add the orzo to the sauce, stir to coat, and season with salt and pepper. Add the orzo and sauce to the baking dish; add water, if necessary, so that the liquid reaches halfway up the sides of the dish.

Bake in the oven, covered with foil, for 25 minutes, or until the orzo is tender. Add hot water to the dish if it gets dry.

While the chicken is in the oven, put the butter in a small saucepan over medium heat. Cook until browned, and add to the chicken after it's been in the oven for 15 minutes.

Serve in the baking dish accompanied by a Simple Green Salad (page 94).

You can make this in a ceramic baking dish with a lid and bake in the oven from the start. Simply place all ingredients except the orzo into the dish and bake until the chicken is tender. Follow the same procedure when adding the orzo.

❀ ❀ ❀

RECETTES
DE
GRAND MÈRE

Briam

OVEN-BAKED VEGETABLES

I saw Kyria Loula for the last time on a Friday. She made me the most amazing briam. It was not chunky and rustic—she had cut all the vegetables into small cubes to make it as refined as possible. This recipe reminds me that, with the passage of time, I am gradually left with fewer people to connect me to a past I haven't known and to people whose meals and lives had built into them the essence of nutrition of body and soul. It makes me feel responsible to preserve, restore, and uphold that which may be lost.   serves • 4 to 5   time • Under 2 hours

2 small potatoes

2 green bell peppers

1 large eggplant

1 leek

2 tomatoes

1 onion, sliced into half moons

2 cloves garlic

½ cup chopped parsley leaves (about ½ bunch)

Extra-virgin olive oil

Salt and pepper

1 tablespoon sugar

½ teaspoon red chili flakes (optional)

Preheat the oven to 350°F (180°C).

Dice the potatoes, bell peppers, eggplant, leek, and tomatoes to roughly the same size, about ½ inch (1 centimeter). Place in a large roasting pan. Combine with the onion, whole garlic cloves, and parsley. Add a generous amount of olive oil, about ⅓ cup (75 milliliters), and toss to coat all the vegetables. Season well with salt, pepper, sugar, and the chili flakes, if using. Pour in about ¾ cup (180 milliliters) of water.

Bake in the oven for 1 hour and 15 minutes. The vegetables should take on a lovely dark color and some should even stick to the edges of the roasting pan. Ensure there's no water, only oil, left in the dish before taking out of the oven.

tip

It's a must to serve briam with a nice chunk of feta cheese!

Intercept the Downfall

*Taste was devised as a method of self-preservation
to detect the potentially harmful and the
potentially nutritive
but today taste has been deceived
now we can engineer something harmful to make it
taste like something nutritive
and the world is upside down*

*eating is a small but huge act intricately connected
to everything
defining us and we defining it.*

*and even if until today we do not know,
it is never late to know*

how to feel full of goodness

Strapatsada

SCRAMBLED EGGS WITH TOMATO SAUCE

This is one of my all-time favorite dishes to eat for dinner on evenings when I don't want to labor over something complicated, but do really want something cozy and tasty to eat. Growing up, we ate this on days when no meal was planned. I enjoyed it even more because it was usually prepared by my mum or dad, who, due to busy work schedules, rarely graced the kitchen with their presence.

serves • 2 to 3   time • Under 30 minutes

1 small onion, finely chopped

Extra-virgin olive oil

Salt and pepper

3 medium tomatoes, grated, or ¾ cup (200 grams) canned diced tomatoes

1 teaspoon sugar

6 large eggs

3 ounces (75 grams) crumbled feta cheese

tip

Be careful when adding salt as feta is a salty cheese.

Add the onion to a frying pan with a thin layer of oil and a pinch of salt. Cook over medium heat until the onion is translucent. Add the tomatoes and sugar with about ½ cup (125 milliliters) of water and let boil for 20 minutes, or until all the juices have evaporated and the mixture has started to caramelize.

Beat the eggs well in a small bowl and season with salt and pepper. Pour into the tomato mixture, lower the heat to medium low, and stir continuously with a wooden spoon. The egg should slowly start to combine with the tomato into one homogeneous mixture—stir continuously to ensure you do not end up with big chunks of cooked egg separate from the sauce.

Once the eggs are cooked, take off the heat and add the feta cheese, mixing well. Serve on toasted bread.

Green Salad with Red Cabbage and Fruits

This is one of two personal contributions I am making to this book. Since salads are one of my favorite things to make, and they were missing from my list of family recipes, I decided to share one of my own with you. Do not forget to observe the intricately beautiful interior of the cabbage and its vibrant color. When I have an extraordinary ingredient such as this in front of me, I imagine the first human being who had the courage to try it, and risked his life for me to be able to use it without fear.   serves • 8 to 10   time • Under 30 minutes

2 heads butter lettuce, washed, torn into bite-size pieces

1 small red cabbage or head of radicchio, shredded

2 ripe avocados, diced

1 tart red apple, diced

1 cup (150 grams) chopped almonds, toasted

¾ cup (180 milliliters) extra-virgin olive oil

⅓ cup (75 milliliters) white balsamic vinegar

1 tablespoon honey

1½ teaspoons Dijon mustard

Salt and pepper

Add the lettuce to a large salad bowl, followed by the cabbage, avocados, apple, and ending with the almonds. Reserve in the fridge.

Combine the oil, vinegar, honey, mustard, salt, and pepper in a jar, cover with the lid, and shake vigorously until you have a homogeneous mixture. Taste and adjust, if necessary: increase acidity by adding some vinegar or mustard; reduce acidity by adding oil; and balance spiciness by adding honey. Making a dressing is a game for your taste buds.

Just before serving, pour about half of the dressing over the salad. Toss gently and taste, adding more dressing as needed. Any leftover dressing will keep, refrigerated, for up to 1 week.

Fakes
LENTIL SOUP

There are some things, like lentil soup, that serve as common ground no matter who you are, and no matter where you are. People from different cultures, people with different eating habits, people with a lot, and people with a little all enjoy a good lentil soup.   serves • 4 to 6   time • Under 2 hours

One 16-ounce (500-gram) package brown lentils

Extra-virgin olive oil

3 tomatoes, grated, or ¾ cup (200 grams) canned diced tomatoes

1 large onion, finely chopped

2 to 3 cloves garlic

2 bay leaves

Salt and pepper

Dried oregano

tip

If the lentils are done but the soup is too thin, remove a cupful of lentils and purée them until smooth, then add back to the pot to thicken the soup.

Boil the lentils in a pot with plenty of water for 5 minutes, then drain. Wipe the pot dry, then cover the bottom with a thin layer of olive oil. Place over medium high heat and add the lentils. Stir to coat in the oil, and add water to cover them generously (about 6 cups / 1.4 liters).

Add the tomatoes, onion, garlic, bay leaves, and pepper. Bring to a boil, then lower the heat and simmer for 40 minutes. Once the lentils are half cooked, season with salt to taste and cook until they are soft, but not mushy.

Before serving, add some olive oil and oregano to taste.

A Protest

Denounce
the industrialization of our food system
the diminishing diversity of seeds
the increase in diversity of products all year round
the huge distance from farm to supermarket
the perfect shape and size and color.

Embrace the process, from growth to
transportation, to cook, to taste
Herald in the modern-day food heroes and
condemn those disrespecting of your right of
access to good-tasting, uncontaminated,
fairly produced food.

Learn more, see more, ask more
Remember a past you have not known and
bring it to the future
Samaritans of food that's good to grow,
Food that's good to sow, the seed for
future generations.

Hide not your faces in the known without
a question as to how and why
Look up, be not afraid to ask or change
the ways you know
Time has a come for things to go astray in
the direction of the opposite good day.

Fasolakia Ladera

GREEN BEANS BRAISED IN OIL

I cannot help but boast about this recipe. I can say with absolute certainty that I have never eaten a better version than the one that is served in my home—and I assure you, there are many people who would testify to this. The secret is in the cutting of the green beans, which end up looking almost like spaghetti. You can either patiently labor over them with a sharp knife or buy a bean slicer to cut and peel them for you. As someone who has done it all by hand multiple times, my advice is to buy the contraption—it is definitely worth the investment!

serves • 6 to 8   time • Under 3 hours

Extra-virgin olive oil

1 large onion, finely chopped

1 large light green pepper, such as Armenian, or ½ green bell pepper, finely chopped

2 pounds (1 kilogram) green beans, trimmed and cut into thin strips

Salt and pepper

¾ cup (180 milliliters) white wine

One 14-ounce (400-gram) can diced tomatoes

2 cups (500 milliliters) Chicken Stock (page 211), Vegetable Stock (page 210), or water

1 teaspoon sugar

1 bay leaf

Add about ½ inch (1 centimeter) of olive oil to a large pot set over medium high heat. Add the onion and green pepper, and cook until the onions are soft and translucent. Add the green beans and salt, cover, and sweat until they have turned a nice dark green. Uncover the pot, add the wine, and reduce until the alcohol has evaporated. Add the tomatoes and boil for 8 minutes to reduce the acidity. Add the stock (or water if you do not have stock), sugar, and bay leaf.

Simmer, uncovered, for about 40 minutes over medium heat until your beans are tasty and soft, and the majority of the liquid has evaporated. Stir occasionally to make sure that your beans have not stuck to the pot (it can happen to the best of us!) and add water if necessary.

Serve with a great big piece of feta and some fresh bread.

tip

To clean the green beans, trim the ends, then use a vegetable peeler to remove the stringy bits from both sides. Or, if you have the bean slicer, let it do the work for you!

Papoutsakia

STUFFED ZUCCHINI

While shopping to test this recipe, I found round zucchini and thought they would be a fun variation to the original dish. Feel free to make this with any type of zucchini you find (to make with regular zucchini, simply cut in half lengthwise); you can also use eggplants, as is common in Greece.

serves • 5 to 6   time • Under 3 hours

6 large globe zucchini

Extra-virgin olive oil

1 tablespoon unsalted butter

1 onion, finely chopped

Salt and pepper

2/3 pound (300 grams) ground beef

6 tablespoons (90 milliliters) white wine

2 tablespoons tomato paste

1 large egg

béchamel

7 tablespoons (100 grams) unsalted butter

3/4 cup (100 grams) all-purpose flour

Generous 3 cups (750 milliliters) milk

Salt and pepper

Ground nutmeg

1/2 cup (60 grams) grated Parmesan cheese

Prepare the zucchini for stuffing by cutting them in half, then scoring a circle around their inside edges.

Bring a large pot of salted water to a boil. Add the zucchini and boil for 5 to 10 minutes, until soft but not cooked through. Drain.

Once cool enough to handle, scoop the flesh out of the zucchini, reserving the shells and placing the flesh in a colander to drain away excess liquid. Chop the zucchini flesh as finely as possible. Lay the zucchini shells in a greased baking dish.

Cover the bottom of a medium frying pan with olive oil and add 1 tablespoon of butter. Place over medium high heat and add the onion and 1 teaspoon salt. Cook until translucent, then add half of the chopped zucchini flesh. (Reserve the other half for an omelet.) Once the zucchini has colored slightly and any excess liquid has evaporated, add the beef, breaking it apart with a wooden spoon. Cook over high heat until browned. Add the white wine, and boil vigorously to let the alcohol evaporate. Stir in the tomato paste and enough water to cover the meat. Boil for 30 minutes, until dry. Take off the heat and, once cool, season with salt and pepper, add the egg, and mix.

Preheat the oven to 350°F (180°C). Make the béchamel, following the instructions on page 216 and using the ingredients listed here.

Stuff each zucchini generously with the meat mixture. Top with a spoonful of béchamel, then with some grated cheese. Bake in the oven for 25 minutes, until the top is golden brown. Serve hot with some feta cheese and a fresh salad.

Fasolada

WHITE BEAN SOUP

I associate this soup with Kyria Loula because, on multiple occasions during my visits to her home in her last days, she repeatedly expressed the desire to have a taste of it. Unfortunately, her stomach was already too weak to digest it, so it will forever remain an unfulfilled wish.   serves • 4 to 6   time • Under 3 hours

One 16-ounce (500-gram) bag dried white beans

Extra-virgin olive oil

1 onion, grated

2 carrots, cut in half lengthwise, then sliced

1 clove garlic, crushed

2 tablespoons tomato paste

1 small celery stalk, sliced

Salt and pepper

1 bay leaf

Red chili flakes

Place the beans in a large pot, cover with water, and bring to a boil. Boil for 10 minutes, then drain and set aside.

Cover the bottom of the same pot with a thin layer of oil and place over medium heat. Add the onion, carrots, and garlic. Cook until the onion is translucent, add the tomato paste, and then add the beans. Stir well to coat the beans in the oil, and add the celery. Cook for 5 minutes, allowing all of the flavors to blend.

Add water to cover the ingredients by about 1 inch (2 centimeters), along with a large pinch of salt and the bay leaf. Bring to a boil, and then lower the heat to a simmer. Continue to simmer gently for 1½ to 2 hours. The beans are ready when they are so full of water that they want to burst. Taste and adjust the salt. Add pepper and chili flakes to taste. Remove the bay leaf and the garlic if you see them swimming around still intact.

Serve in a soup bowl, with some leaves of baby lettuce, Taramosalata (page 152), smoked herring, black olives, feta, and fresh bread.

Chicken Milaneza

This dish was not one of my favorites growing up. I disliked the lemony flavor and associated it with being ill, since it was made when my mother wanted to nourish us with a well-rounded, easily digestible meal. But it was always a favorite in my cousins' home. I include this dish for them, for me, and for you because I have come to appreciate the nourishing quality for which it was cherished in my house and am sure both you and I will be using it when needed.

serves • 4 to 6   time • Under 2 hours

1 whole free-range chicken, about 4 pounds (2 kilograms)

4 whole cloves

1 large onion, peeled and left whole

2 large carrots

1 bouquet garni (see tip, below)

Salt and pepper

Extra-virgin olive oil

1½ cups (280 grams) uncooked basmati rice

1 tablespoon unsalted butter

1 tablespoon cornstarch

1 large egg yolk

Juice of ½ lemon

tip

To make a bouquet garni, cut a 2-inch (5-centimeter) length from the white part of a leek. Peel the outer layer off and fill the center with parsley, a bay leaf or sprig of thyme, and whole black peppercorns. Fold in the sides of the leek as you would a present and tie it with a piece of string or twine.

Wash the chicken and pat dry. Stick the cloves into the onion.

Place the chicken in a large pot along with the onion, carrots, bouquet garni, and salt. Add water to barely cover the ingredients. Bring to a boil, reduce the heat, and simmer about 45 minutes, until cooked through. After about 30 minutes, check to see if the carrots are cooked through; if so, remove them and set aside.

Take the chicken off the heat and let cool in the cooking liquid. Once cool, remove the chicken from the stock and either shred it or cut it into pieces. Strain the stock through a fine-mesh sieve. Place the chicken in a dish and cover with a little stock to keep it from drying out.

Reserve 1 cup (250 milliliters) of stock for the sauce and use the rest for the rice.

Cover the bottom of a medium pot with a thin layer of oil. Place over low heat, then add the rice. Heat until the rice starts turning a rosy color, stirring often so that it doesn't burn. Add the stock to reach ½ inch (1 centimeter) above the rice; if there isn't enough stock, top with water. Bring to a boil and boil vigorously for 5 minutes, then turn the burner to the lowest possible heat, cover with a lid, and cook for 20 to 25 minutes, until the rice is tender and fragrant.

Continued

Make the sauce, just as you would a béchamel. Start by melting the butter in a small saucepan over medium heat. Add the cornstarch and mix well. Pour in the cup (250 milliliters) of reserved stock, whisking constantly until it thickens.

Lower the heat substantially and add the egg yolk, whisking constantly. Season with salt and pepper. Gradually add the lemon juice. Once ready, leave the sauce on the stove on the lowest setting in order to keep it warm.

Place the chicken and carrots in a medium pot along with the stock to reheat. Let the stock reach a simmer and move the pot around to stir the ingredients and prevent burning. Once warmed through, take off the heat and drain.

Serve on a platter, starting with a layer of rice, then the chicken and a few spoonfuls of sauce. Decorate with the boiled carrots, cut into thick rounds. Place any remaining sauce in a sauceboat to serve at the table.

Lahano Karoto

CABBAGE AND CARROT SALAD

I find it humorous to write a recipe for this salad, as there is nothing very technical about grating cabbage and carrots and combining them with olive oil, vinegar, and salt. Yet if it did not appear in this cookbook, the thought of making it might never occur to you. The presence of this recipe is symbolic: it is not only the complicated that I wish to glorify in this book, but also the simple. Do not try to make it beautiful, but do find the beauty in its simplicity.

serves • 4 to 6   time • Under 30 minutes

1 small green cabbage, grated

4 carrots, grated

¾ cup (180 milliliters) extra-virgin olive oil, or to taste

¼ cup (60 milliliters) white wine vinegar, or to taste

Salt

Toss the cabbage and carrots together in a bowl, then drizzle with olive oil and vinegar, and season with salt. Taste to ensure there's the right balance between the olive oil and vinegar, adding more of either one if needed. Toss again, and serve.

Lavraki Plaki

OVEN-BAKED SEA BASS

This dish is not one that I grew up with, but Kyria Loula and I decided it was a good one to include because it is so simple and easy to make. The only thing you need to plan is going to the fishmonger to buy a fresh fish. You can cook it whole or in fillets, depending on your preference. Either way, ask the fishmonger to clean it for you. It is important to establish good relationships with those providing the ingredients you bring into your kitchen and serve on your table. So, if you haven't already, ask around for the best place to buy fish, and find out all you can about the fish you are about to cook: where it is from, whether it was raised on a farm or swam free in the sea, when it was caught, and how.

serves • 2 to 3   time • Under 1 hour

Salt and pepper

1 sea bass, about 2 pounds (1 kilogram), filleted or left whole

1 pound (500 grams) potatoes, peeled

Extra-virgin olive oil

1 onion, sliced in half moons

6 medium tomatoes, diced, or one 14-ounce (400-gram) can diced tomatoes

1 clove garlic, crushed

1 tablespoon dried thyme, oregano, or rosemary

1½ teaspoons ground cumin

1 teaspoon sugar

tip

You can substitute cod or sea bream, among others, for the sea bass.

Salt the fish generously and let it sit in the fridge while you make the sauce. Cut the potatoes into 2-inch-long-by-1-inch-wide (5-centimeters-long-by-2.5-centimeters-wide) pieces and place in a medium bowl. Cover with cold water.

Coat a medium frying pan with a generous amount of olive oil. Place over medium high heat, add the onion, and cook until translucent and just starting to take color. Add the tomatoes, garlic, thyme, cumin, sugar, salt, and pepper. Simmer for about 10 minutes, then add the potatoes and a cupful (250 milliliters) of water, and continue cooking for about 20 minutes.

Preheat the oven to 390°F (200°C).

Lay the fish in a baking dish and pour the sauce over it, scattering the potatoes around the sides. Add another cupful (250 milliliters) of water to reach halfway up the potatoes and just about cover the fish.

Bake in the oven for 30 minutes. Add water as needed so the dish never goes dry. If the potatoes need more time than the fish, remove the fish and put on a plate, and return the potatoes to the oven for a few minutes more. Serve in the baking dish or on a platter you love!

Arakas

OIL-STEWED GREEN PEAS

This is one of the thirty-some-odd recipes that were missing from my list when Kyria Loula decided she had left enough of her cooking legacy with me and departed without a word of warning. When I went to my great-aunt's house to retrieve the recipes I didn't get the chance to collect from Kyria Loula, she told me that I could make this dish with or without tomato sauce. Despite having eaten peas stewed in tomato sauce all my life, I decided to try them stewed only in oil. It turns out that they are delicious when cooked this way, too, so I have provided the oil-stewed recipe here, with the optional addition of tomatoes.

Serve to accompany a meal or eat it alone with some good feta and a poached or fried egg on top for an extremely satisfying dinner.

serves • 2 to 4   time • Under 1 hour

Extra-virgin olive oil

1 onion, finely chopped

1 pound (500 grams) shelled peas

¾ cup chopped dill (about ½ bunch)

Salt and pepper

tomato sauce (optional)

¾ cup (200 grams) canned diced tomatoes

1 teaspoon sugar

2 medium carrots, cut into thin rounds

In a medium pot, heat 2 tablespoons olive oil. Add the onion and a splash of water, and cook until the onion is translucent. If you'd like a red sauce, add the tomatoes, sugar, and carrots. Add the peas and give them a toss in the oil. Add half the dill, a pinch of salt and pepper, and then enough water to just cover the peas.

Bring to a boil and then turn the heat down to a gentle simmer. Cook, covered, for about 40 minutes, checking the pan every once in a while in case it needs more water. The peas are ready once they're soft but firm. Once off the heat, add the rest of the dill.

Serve hot or cold with a drizzle of olive oil to taste. (I prefer eating these peas at room temperature.)

Substitute frozen peas for fresh ones if you are really craving this out of season.

Moussaka

Moussaka is as synonymous with Greece as the Acropolis. Yet, unlike the fixed appearance and position of the ancient temple, there is no universal experience of moussaka. Greeks living within Greece turn to their *giagia* or *mama* for a taste of it, and the taste is unique to each home. Tourists eat a version of it in the Greek *taverna* that usually looks right but tastes wrong. Others have taken the liberty to meddle with it, serving their creative interpretations in restaurants worldwide. Greek immigrants eat it to remind themselves of home and pass it on to second and third generations of their family as a declaration of their Greekness.

So what is it that this unofficial emblem of Greece represents, if every person experiences it differently? If moussaka represents Greece only in one's mental capacity, then we must let go of it as an emblem. Perhaps the deconstructed identity of a modern-day Greek man or woman lies deep in the center of a moussaka.   serves • 6 to 8   time • Under 3 hours

3 large or 5 medium eggplants, sliced lengthwise

Salt and pepper

2 large potatoes, peeled and cut lengthwise into ¼-inch (5-millimeter) slices

Extra-virgin olive oil

Sugar

1 recipe Kimas (page 217)

béchamel

7 tablespoons (100 grams) unsalted butter

¾ cup (100 grams) all-purpose flour

Generous 3 cups (750 milliliters) milk

3 tablespoons heavy cream

Salt and pepper

Ground nutmeg

Melted butter or extra-virgin olive oil, for greasing

1½ cups (170 grams) grated cheese, such as Graviera or Gruyère

Preheat the oven to 350°F (180°C).

Place the eggplant slices in a colander and sprinkle generously with salt. Put the colander in the sink, or place a plate underneath it to catch the bitter juice released by the eggplants. Let sit for 30 minutes.

Rinse the eggplants. Lay the slices in a single layer on baking sheets lined with parchment paper. Do the same with the potato slices. Brush both the potatoes and eggplants with olive oil and season with salt and pepper. Sprinkle each eggplant slice with a little sugar. Bake in the oven for 35 minutes, or until they start taking some color and are cooked through.

Make the kimas as instructed on page 217.

Make the béchamel following the instructions on page 216 and using the ingredients listed here.

Assemble the moussaka by brushing the bottom of a 13-by-9-inch (33-by-23-centimeter) baking dish with melted butter or olive oil, then sprinkling with a thin layer of grated cheese. Add a single layer of potatoes, cover with a layer of half the eggplants, then kimas, grated cheese, remaining eggplants, grated cheese, béchamel, and a little grated cheese to finish. Make sure each layer is seasoned to taste.

Bake in the oven for 35 to 40 minutes, until the top is golden brown.

This dish can be assembled in advance. Freeze before baking, then defrost for 6 hours before putting in the oven.

Stuffed Crêpe Cannelloni

There are two things that excite me about this recipe: making the crêpes, and eating the leftover crêpes after dinner, rolled up with strawberry jam, just as we did on Monday nights. Kyria Loula cooked all our weekly meals on Mondays, and if there was cannelloni on the menu, there were also leftover crêpes.

serves • 4 to 5   time • Under 3 hours

crêpes

3 large eggs

¾ cup (100 grams) all-purpose flour

Generous 1½ cups (375 milliliters) milk

Salt and pepper

1 tablespoon unsalted butter, melted

1 recipe Kimas (page 217)

béchamel

1½ tablespoons unsalted butter

1½ tablespoons all-purpose flour

Generous 1¾ cups (450 milliliters) milk

Salt and pepper

Pinch ground nutmeg

3½ tablespoons heavy cream (optional)

Extra-virgin olive oil

Handful grated Graviera or Parmesan cheese

Start by making the crêpe batter. Whisk the eggs with the flour until smooth. Keep whisking and add the milk, a pinch of salt, and the melted butter. Let the mixture sit for 1 hour in the fridge until it thickens slightly.

While the batter chills, make the kimas as instructed on page 217. Set aside to cool.

Make the béchamel, following the instructions on page 216 and using the butter, flour, and milk amounts listed here. Season with salt, pepper, and nutmeg and, once off the heat, whisk in some cream if it needs thinning.

Now take a small frying pan (about 6 inches / 15 centimeters across), brush it lightly with oil, and heat it up. Pour in half a ladle of crêpe batter, and immediately swirl and tilt the pan so that the batter evenly covers the bottom. Pour any excess mixture back into the bowl of batter. Lift one edge of the crêpe with the back of a teaspoon—if it easily slides off the frying pan and has taken on a little color, it is ready to flip. Use your fingers to do this—it requires practice and patience. The first one or two always go to waste; don't be discouraged. Once the other side has cooked, place the crêpe on a plate. Repeat with the rest of the batter.

Preheat the oven to 350°F (180°C).

To make the cannelloni: Set up your work station with a plate or cutting board in the center, and the crêpes, a greased baking dish, and the kimas to the sides. Place a crêpe on the plate or cutting board, add

1 tablespoon of kimas to the center of the crêpe, and roll up halfway. Fold in the edges and roll up completely.

Place in the baking dish with the seam of the crêpe facing down. Repeat with the remaining ingredients.

Pour the béchamel over the cannelloni, sprinkle with the grated cheese, and bake in the oven for 30 minutes, or until golden on top.

tip

Use any leftover kimas to make scrambled eggs. Eat any leftover crêpes for breakfast or an afternoon snack, with jam, sugar, or praline spread—or freeze them to enjoy later.

Kotopoulo sto Fourno

CHICKEN IN THE OVEN

This dish inherently calls out to be shared. I tried on various occasions to serve it at my own table without much success, because I always made up the recipe as I went along. Though my imagination thrived and something new was born, it always lacked the roots I was looking to share with those who had never tasted the dish. I was surprised to see that if I followed a recipe and impersonated an old Greek woman in the kitchen, using more oil than necessary, feeling more round than I am, and channeling a mother's instinct, I could make the chicken taste just the way I remember it. <u>serves</u> · 4 to 6   <u>time</u> · Under 2 hours

1 whole free-range chicken, about 4 pounds (2 kilograms)

Extra-virgin olive oil

2 to 3 tablespoons unsalted butter

Salt and pepper

1 large lemon

Dried oregano

4 medium potatoes, peeled and quartered

Preheat the oven to 325°F (170°C).

Wash the chicken and pat dry. Place in a roasting pan or dish, drizzle generously with olive oil, and rub it all over. Use a knife to make 4 to 5 slits in the skin and insert a small piece of butter in each slit, between the skin and the meat.

Mix together some salt and pepper and season the chicken well, including the inside cavity. Cut the lemon in half and juice it, retaining both the juice and one of the lemon halves. Stuff the cavity of the chicken with the one half of the squeezed lemon and a teaspoon of butter. Sprinkle the top with oregano and add some to the baking dish as well. Pour half the lemon juice into the dish along with ½ cup (125 milliliters) of water and ¼ cup (60 milliliters) of olive oil. Cover with foil.

Bake in the oven for 45 minutes. Add the potatoes and season well with salt, pepper, and oregano. Taste the juices that have collected in the dish, and add more lemon juice to taste. Add more water to nearly cover the potatoes and cook, covered with foil, for another 45 minutes. Check on the chicken from time to time to see if it needs water, and stir the potatoes each time.

When the chicken's juices run clear and the potatoes are soft, remove the foil, increase the oven's temperature to 425°F (220°C), and roast for 5 to 7 minutes, until the chicken skin takes on some color and gets a little crispy. Most of the water should have evaporated, leaving behind a thin sauce. Before serving, use a good knife to cut the chicken into pieces. Serve in the baking dish with a fork and a large spoon to scoop up the tasty sauce.

Cheese and Ham on Toast, Topped with a Fried Egg

This is one of my eldest cousin Alexia's most cherished recipes, and it perfectly illustrates the value of a childhood food memory. I can only assume that it is not the dish itself that makes this taste worth keeping in her memory, but rather what she felt when her mother made it on a Sunday night. As a working mother, my aunt rarely had the time to cook dinner for the family; this dish has been endowed forever with the magical ability to re-create that warm feeling of being fed by food cooked by our mothers. Alexia has vowed to keep this tradition alive and share this recipe with her young daughters today.

serves • 1   time • Under 30 minutes

Unsalted butter

1 slice bread (whatever kind you like)

1 to 2 slices good-quality boiled ham

2 to 3 slices Emmental or Gruyère cheese

Extra-virgin olive oil

1 large egg

Salt and pepper

Preheat the oven to 375°F (190°C).

Spread a thin layer of butter on the bread. Layer with ham and then cheese. Place on a baking sheet and put in the oven for 10 to 15 minutes, until the cheese melts and starts to brown.

Meanwhile, heat about ½ inch (1 centimeter) of olive oil in a small frying pan over medium heat. Crack in the egg and fry to your desired doneness, spooning hot oil from the frying pan over the top of the egg to help it cook.

Once the ham and cheese toast is ready, transfer to a plate and lay the egg on top of it. Season with salt and pepper. Serve hot.

Pasta Flora

JAM TART

I have found that if I am to be at peace, I must have a multidimensional relationship with food, just as it was in my home, and many other Greek homes, when I was growing up. Some days we were carnivores, others we were vegetarians or vegans; sometimes we were very healthy and other times not; but we didn't need to be any of these things forever.

Pasta flora seemed like an appropriate recipe to accompany these thoughts, as the lattice design on top that separates the jam into squares reminds me of the way I, and other humans, often sort our life into boxes.

serves · 6 to 8   time · Under 2 hours

**1 Sweet Pastry Case
(page 219)**

**²/₃ cup (150 grams) Apricot Jam
(page 190)**

tip

If the dough breaks on the way to the pan, don't worry. Fill in the holes with extra pastry, pressing it down with your fingers.

Make the sweet pastry case dough as instructed on page 219. Wrap in parchment paper and let sit in the fridge for at least 30 minutes.

Preheat the oven to 375°F (190°C).

Take three-quarters of the dough and soften it with your hands. Dust your work surface with flour and roll the dough out to an 11-inch (28-centimeter) round about ¼ inch (5 millimeters) thick. (Do not add too much flour as it will make the dough dry.) Roll it around the rolling pin and unroll it over a round tart pan, about 10 inches (25 centimeters) in diameter. Use your fingers to gently fit the dough into the pan.

Using the back of a spoon, spread the apricot jam over the base. Add more or less jam to taste. If the apricot jam is too thick, dilute it with water until easily spreadable.

Now soften the rest of the dough, roll it out to approximately 6 inches (15 centimeters) square, and cut 14 long strips out of it. Take one strip at a time and roll it between your hands to make a snake. Lay 7 on top of the tart in one direction and 7 in the other direction, in even intervals, to form a lattice pattern.

Bake in the oven for 30 to 35 minutes, or until the jam turns a dark orange color and the pastry is golden brown. Let cool before serving.

Semolina Halva

This recipe is not one with a story from my past—rather, it is a recipe for an essential Greek dessert that I have only recently acquired a taste for. It is dairy-free, and you can substitute the sugar with other sweeteners and adjust the level of sweetness according to your preference.   <u>serves</u> • 4 to 6   <u>time</u> • Under 1 hour

½ cup (120 milliliters) extra-virgin olive oil

1⅔ cups (280 grams) coarse semolina

1¼ cups (250 grams) granulated sugar

1 tablespoon honey

1 cinnamon stick

1¼ cups (120 grams) chopped almonds, toasted

¾ cup (100 grams) golden raisins

tip

If you wish to serve the halva in slices, pack it into a 13-by-9-inch (33-by-23-centimeter) cake pan while it's still hot and cover with a tea towel. Once cool, invert it onto a serving platter and slice into pieces.

Pour the oil and the semolina into a deep frying pan or medium saucepan over medium heat. Using a wooden spoon, mix until the semolina has completely absorbed the oil. Keep mixing slowly, pausing every so often to allow the semolina to take on color. (The semolina will start going from golden to light brown as it cooks.) Do not let the mixture cook too quickly; turn the heat down to medium low if needed. Cook the semolina for 20 to 30 minutes, stirring until it takes on a light brown tint.

Meanwhile, make the syrup: Combine the sugar, honey, and cinnamon stick with a generous 3 cups (750 milliliters) of water in a large saucepan and bring to a boil. Boil for 5 minutes, then remove from the heat.

When the semolina is ready, remove the cinnamon stick from the syrup and bring back to a boil. Add the almonds and raisins to the semolina, and remove from the heat. Pour in the hot syrup, carefully, as it spits the moment it comes into contact with the hot pan. Step away from the pan while it does this, and give it a good stir once it stops spattering.

Place the pan of semolina back over low heat and stir, making sure the syrup is absorbed. The halva is ready when it is one homogeneous mixture that easily slides off the sides of the pan. The texture should be crumbly, not thick and sticky. Take off the heat, cover with a tea towel, and let cool.

Fluff the halva with a fork and place in a serving bowl.

Crème Caramel

I recall my brother loving this dessert much more than I did growing up, but he remembers hating it! It doesn't really matter whose memory is right; today I feel that a home kitchen without a crème caramel recipe is incomplete. Words cannot explain why. Just make it, and you will understand.

serves · 4 to 6   time · Under 2 hours

Generous 2 cups
   (500 milliliters) milk

Scant ½ cup (100 milliliters)
   heavy cream

1 cinnamon stick

1 large strip of lemon zest

1¼ cups (250 grams)
   granulated sugar

5 large eggs

Remember two things: not to burn yourself, and not to burn the caramel—it can go from golden to dark brown in the blink of an eye!

Combine the milk and cream in a saucepan over low heat. Add the cinnamon stick and lemon zest, and allow to infuse. Remove from the heat just before the milk starts to bubble.

In a small pan over medium high heat, combine ¾ cup (150 grams) of the sugar and 7 tablespoons (100 milliliters) water. Bring to a boil and cook until the sugar has melted and the mixture has turned a dark golden brown. Immediately pour the hot caramel into either a loaf pan or among individual ramekins. Tilt to ensure the bottom is completely covered with the caramel.

Preheat the oven to 350°F (180°C). Line a large roasting pan with a tea towel, and place the prepared loaf pan or ramekins on top.

Strain the milk mixture, discarding the lemon zest and cinnamon stick. Beat the eggs with the remaining ½ cup (100 grams) sugar. Still mixing, slowly add the warm milk. Pour into the prepared loaf pan or ramekins, then pour hot water into the roasting pan a third of the way up the sides of the loaf pan or ramekins.

Bake in the oven for 40 minutes if using a loaf pan. If you're using ramekins, start checking at 20 minutes. Test for doneness by sticking a knife in the center—it should come out clean. Cool completely, then invert onto a plate or platter to serve.

Mosaico

I have loved this dessert ever since I was young. I remember sneaking slices off the roll we had wrapped up in the freezer throughout the day. It is something that can either be served as an easy dessert for guests, or made and kept in the freezer to satisfy a sweet craving at any time of the day.

<u>serves</u> • 8 to 10   <u>time</u> • Under 3 hours

1 cup (2 sticks / 225 grams) unsalted butter, room temperature

³/₄ cup (150 grams) granulated sugar

3 large eggs

4¹/₂ tablespoons unsweetened cocoa powder

1 teaspoon vanilla extract

14 ounces (400 grams) butter cookies, such as petit beurre or animal crackers, broken up into small pieces

Beat together the butter and sugar. While beating, add the eggs one at a time, followed by the cocoa and vanilla.

Add the cookie pieces and mix with a spoon until all the pieces seem to be surrounded evenly by chocolate—you may think the chocolate is not enough but trust me, it is!

Spoon into a cake pan or 9-by-5-inch (23-by-13-centimeter) loaf pan that's been lined with parchment paper. Press the mixture down into the pan to compact it and make it even, then fold the excess parchment paper over the top to cover the chocolate mixture completely.

Freeze for at least 2 hours before serving. To serve, take out of the pan and slice into thick pieces. Arrange on a cutting board or on a fancy plate.

tip

Make sure to put the batter in the freezer immediately once it is ready, as it contains raw egg. Once all your guests are served, wrap any leftovers with parchment paper and put them back in the freezer.

tip

If you have left the mosaico in the freezer for much more than 2 hours, make sure you take it out of the freezer at least 15 minutes before serving.

Orange Cake and Marble Cake

In my first cousins' childhood home, one of my cousins preferred orange cake, one preferred marble, and the third was too young to have a say. The solution was to alternate, until one day someone had the wonderful idea to bake both at once in the same pan. With this solution, both cousins got their way and neither of them felt less loved.   serves • 8 to 10   time • Under 2 hours

11 tablespoons (150 grams) unsalted butter, room temperature, plus more for greasing

2½ cups (320 grams) all-purpose flour, plus more for dusting

1 scant cup (180 grams) granulated sugar

4 large eggs, separated

Zest of 3 oranges

1 teaspoon vanilla extract

¼ cup plus 2 tablespoons (90 milliliters) milk

¼ cup plus 2 tablespoons (90 milliliters) orange juice

1 tablespoon baking powder

Pinch salt

2 heaping tablespoons unsweetened cocoa powder

Preheat the oven to 375°F (190°C). Butter a 9-by-3-inch (23-by-8-centimeter) Bundt pan or 9-by-5-inch (23-by-13-centimeter) loaf pan and dust with flour.

Using an electric mixer, cream the butter and sugar. Beat in one egg yolk at a time, then add the orange zest and vanilla, continuing to beat on medium speed.

Combine the milk and orange juice in a small bowl and mix well. Stir the baking powder into the flour. While mixing on a low speed, alternately add the flour mixture and the milk mixture to the butter mixture.

Beat the egg whites, with a pinch of salt, to stiff peaks. Fold the egg whites into the cake mixture with a spatula. Fold in gently so the mixture doesn't lose volume. Pour three-quarters of the mixture into the prepared pan. Add the cocoa powder to the remaining mixture, and mix until well combined. Pour the chocolate batter over the batter in the pan. Insert a fork into the mixture until you reach the bottom of the pan, and swirl it around to make sure the chocolate goes everywhere.

Bake in the oven for 35 minutes without opening the oven. Test for doneness by inserting a knife into the center—if it comes out clean, your cake is ready. If not, bake for another 5 minutes and check again.

Remove the cake from the oven and allow to cool slightly in the pan. Then carefully invert the cake onto a cooling rack to cool completely.

Sundays

Every Sunday as I was growing up we met religiously at my grandmother's for lunch with the family. The lunches built in me a sense of belonging within a clan of wildly different people with a similar set of elementary values. It is among family that I began to relate to others in the most basic of ways; subconsciously, family became a wall off which I could bounce things, if only to see how they would bounce back.

I cannot remember the exact dishes we ate at these Sunday gatherings so much as the atmosphere surrounding them, so I have built this chapter on the food I imagine we ate, the food I remember eating when we had guests at home, and the food we eat today when we meet for Sunday lunch.

What I do remember clearly is running into my grandmother's kitchen with my brother and cousins the moment we arrived, and her shooing us out so as not to get in the way of the cooking; the frozen fried potatoes that were the exception to everything I was being taught about food; my youngest cousin eating way less savory food than what was deemed appropriate to save room for more dessert, and my grandmother scolding her for doing so; and how sad and lonely it felt when the family gatherings started getting smaller, as each of us entered new stages of our lives.

These dishes take a substantial amount of preparation; one must not rush through the steps, but instead take time to enjoy the process, turning the kitchen into the most exciting place to be in the house. After all, it is here that the magic is stirred.

What is sacred to me about Sunday lunch today, and what makes it a tradition I wish to continue, is that time stops—for a few hours we are excused from all productive activity and obligations beyond spending time together as a family.

Hunkiar Beyendi

BEEF STEW WITH SMOKED EGGPLANT PURÉE

I dedicate this beef stew to Giagia Sofia, the instigator of all our Sunday gatherings, as I remember being introduced to it at her house on a Sunday, and I believe she loved eating it herself. I wrote something for her that you can find on page 226—in it, I hope to communicate the extent of her charisma to those who never met her.   serves · 4 to 6   time · Under 3 hours

2 pounds (1 kilogram) boneless beef brisket or shank, cut into 1-inch (2-centimeter) pieces

Salt and pepper

2 onions

3 whole cloves

Extra-virgin olive oil

2 cloves garlic, crushed

3/4 cup (180 milliliters) red wine

1 tablespoon tomato paste

1 cinnamon stick

1 bay leaf

6 medium tomatoes, grated, or one 14-ounce (400-gram) can diced tomatoes

1 1/2 teaspoons sugar

3 pounds (1.5 kilograms) eggplants

2 tablespoons unsalted butter

2 tablespoons all-purpose flour

1 3/4 cups (400 milliliters) milk

1/3 cup (80 grams) grated Graviera or Parmesan cheese

Ground nutmeg

Season the beef with salt. Peel one of the onions and stick the cloves into it. Finely chop the other onion. Line a large pot with about 1/2 inch (1 centimeter) olive oil, and heat until nearly smoking. Add the beef and brown on all sides. Remove and set aside on a plate.

Add the chopped onion, the whole onion, and the garlic to the oil. Reduce the heat to medium, and cook until the onions are golden. Add the wine and allow to boil until all the alcohol has evaporated, turning up the heat if necessary.

Add the beef back to the pot, along with any juices that have accumulated on the plate. Add the tomato paste, cinnamon stick, bay leaf, and some pepper. Add water to barely cover the meat.

Bring to a boil, then cover, reduce to a simmer, and cook for 1 1/2 hours. Check occasionally and add water if needed. Add the grated tomatoes, season to taste, and cook for another hour, uncovered, on low heat. Taste, season, and add the sugar.

While the meat cooks, prepare the smoked eggplant purée. Pierce the eggplants all over, then smoke by holding them over a gas burner, broiling them in the oven, or adding them to an old frying pan with no oil over high heat (you'll want to use an old frying pan here because the charred bits are hard to scrub off—even after soaking for ages!). Ensure the skins are completely burned on all sides by leaving each side on the heat for the same amount of time.

Once charred, scoop the flesh out of each eggplant. Don't worry if small pieces of skin get included. Drain the flesh in a fine-mesh sieve with a bowl placed under it to collect the juices.

Make a béchamel: Melt the butter in a saucepan over medium heat and add the flour all at once. Stir with a wooden spoon. Once golden, whisk in the milk and the eggplant juice. Cook for 20 minutes on low heat, stirring often with the whisk, until it becomes a thick béchamel. Remove from the heat and add the grated cheese and season to taste with salt, pepper, and nutmeg. Chop the eggplant flesh up and add to the béchamel. Season again to taste.

Remove the whole onion, cinnamon stick, and bay leaf from the beef stew before serving. Make a mound of eggplant purée on a platter and top with the beef.

For an even tastier version, buy osso buco and cook it with the bone. Remove the bone right before serving.

Kotopita

CHICKEN PIE

My great-aunt, who is the orchestrator of our extended family gatherings these days, gave me the recipe for this pie; it is her specialty. When sharing the recipe, she displayed a mix of pride and gentle arrogance, and her eyes shone bright with the idea of this dish being attempted in a kitchen far away from hers. All of the cooks I approached to collect the recipes for this book displayed similar reactions to hers: once they realized I was genuinely interested, they were off—explaining, remembering, and hesitating when they thought my culinary background could bring into question their age-old techniques.

serves · 8 to 10   time · Under 3 hours

1½ pounds (750 grams) bone-in chicken pieces or 1 small whole free-range chicken

1½ pounds (750 grams) onions, quartered

Salt

8 black peppercorns

2 tablespoons unsalted butter

1½ cups (150 grams) grated Parmesan cheese

1 tablespoon semolina

8 large eggs, beaten

¼ cup (60 milliliters) milk or cream

Extra-virgin olive oil

One 8-ounce (225-gram) package phyllo dough

If using the whole chicken, wash it and pat dry. Put the chicken and the onions in a large pot, add 1 tablespoon of salt and the peppercorns. Add enough water to half-cover the chicken, and bring to a boil. Cook, covered, until the onions start softening, then simmer, uncovered, until the onions are so soft they disintegrate and there is no more than a ladleful of water left. Remove the chicken from the pot, reserving the onions and cooking liquid, and shred the meat once cool enough to handle. Discard the skin and bones.

Melt the butter in a large frying pan over medium heat. Add the shredded chicken, the disintegrated onions, and the cooking liquid. Simmer for 5 minutes, then remove from the heat and add the Parmesan, semolina, eggs, milk or cream, and salt to taste. Make sure that the filling is juicy and moist—do not worry about it making the phyllo soggy, as it has enough eggs to pull it together.

Preheat the oven to 350°F (180°C).

Brush a 13-by-9-inch (33-by-23-centimeter) baking dish or pan with olive oil. Start the pie by laying a phyllo sheet on all four sides of the baking dish. Each sheet should partially cover the bottom of the dish, with the rest hanging over the edge. Brush every piece of phyllo that you lay on the dish with oil. Then place five sheets in the center, brushing each with oil. Add the filling and spread it out evenly.

Place five more sheets of phyllo over the filling, then fold over the overhanging sheets that you started with. Cut any excess phyllo away with scissors or a knife and use your pastry brush to tuck the phyllo in around the edges of the dish. Score the top with a sharp knife, marking the pieces you wish to cut later. Sprinkle with a little water.

Bake in the oven for about 1 hour, until the phyllo is golden brown.

Kotopoulo Lemonato

LEMON CHICKEN STEW

When Kyria Loula gave me this recipe, my incredulity was noticeable. "Really?" I said. "Is it that simple?" She was offended, thinking I doubted she was giving me the correct recipe. She couldn't seem to understand that my disbelief stemmed from the realization that something so delectable could be so easy to make!

Miscommunications like this are inevitable in life, and bridging the gap is not always possible. Kyria Loula and Giagia Sofia had a special relationship, one that was often fraught with miscommunication. The combination of the former's habit of taking things way too personally and the latter's unlimited provision of unfiltered criticism bred fertile ground for a lot of affection and conflict. For the rest of us, this was often just a source of entertainment.

serves • 4 to 6   time • Under 2 hours

1 whole free-range chicken, about 4 pounds (2 kilograms), cut into pieces

Salt and pepper

All-purpose flour, for dusting

Extra-virgin olive oil

1 large onion, finely chopped

¾ cup (180 milliliters) white wine

Chicken Stock (page 211) or water, as needed

Juice of 1 lemon

Wash the chicken and pat dry. Season the chicken with salt and pepper and dust well with flour. Cover the bottom of a large pot with olive oil. Heat over medium high heat and, once hot, add the chicken, and brown on all sides. Remove the chicken and set aside.

Add the onion to the pot and lower the heat to medium. Cook until translucent, then return the chicken to the pot. Add the white wine and boil until the alcohol has evaporated. Add enough stock or water to barely cover the chicken.

Simmer, partially covered, on low heat for 1 hour. Check and add water if needed. When the liquid is one-quarter of its original volume, uncover, add half of the lemon juice, and cook until the sauce has thickened. Adjust the lemon juice to taste.

Serve hot with fried or baked potatoes and feta cheese!

Accordion Potatoes

These potatoes are as exciting to eat as they are to prepare. They are crunchy on the outside, like chips, and soft at the center, like baked potatoes.

If you want to be frugal, strain the leftover oil to remove all the burned bits, then store in a glass jar to use the next time you want to fry something. I suggest using it no more than twice.   serves • 4 to 5   time • Under 2 hours

7 medium potatoes, peeled

1 cup (250 milliliters) extra-virgin olive oil

⅓ cup (75 milliliters) sunflower oil

Salt and pepper

Juice of ½ lemon

Choose similar-size potatoes, preferably oval and flat.

Place two chopsticks along the horizontal sides of the potato like railroad tracks while cutting to prevent slicing all the way through it.

Place a potato on a cutting board on the side that feels most stable. Using a large sharp knife, make slices into it without cutting all the way through so that by the end it looks a little like an accordion. (Take a look at the photo opposite—it will help guide you!)

Preheat the oven to 350°F (180°C).

Once all of the potatoes are sliced, place them neatly in a baking dish, and pour the oil around and in between the slices of each potato. Season generously with salt and pepper. Bake in the oven for 1 hour, then turn the oven temperature up to 450°F (230°C) and pour a little lemon juice over each potato. Bake for another 25 minutes.

Lift each potato out of the oil, stopping to dab on a paper towel to absorb the excess oil before placing on a plate to serve.

Lahanodolmades

STUFFED CABBAGE LEAVES

The taste of lahanodolmades is so distinct and specific that the first time I made them I was shocked to find I had cooked something that tasted exactly like it had been made by an experienced Greek grandma. As I consider myself far from traditional, I found this realization extremely reassuring. I would be remiss if I did not warn you that this dish requires time, patience, and a strong desire to share it.   serves · 6 to 8   time · 4 hours or longer

1 large green cabbage

Extra-virgin olive oil

1 large onion, finely chopped

1 pound (500 grams) ground beef

½ pound (250 grams) ground pork

Scant 1 cup (200 grams) Greek yogurt

6 tablespoons uncooked short-grain rice

1 large egg

¾ cup chopped dill (about 1 bunch)

1 tablespoon dried mint

Salt and pepper

1 pork or beef rib bone

1 recipe Avgolemono (page 215)

Bring a large pot of salted water to a boil. Cut the cabbage in half and cut out the thick core.

Once the water is boiling, add one half of the cabbage. The outer leaves will be ready first, so when they start to peel off and look translucent, remove them and lay them on a large plate. Repeat this process until all the leaves are cooked, then repeat with the other half.

Heat a generous drizzle of olive oil in a frying pan over medium high heat. Add the onion and cook until golden. Transfer to a mixing bowl along with the beef, pork, yogurt, rice, egg, herbs, salt, and pepper. Mix with your hands until all the ingredients are well combined.

Place a cutting board in front of you and lay out one cabbage leaf. If part of the core is still attached, cut it out. Put a small teaspoon of filling at the base of the leaf, fold over, tuck in the sides, then roll to the other edge. This technique takes practice and each cook finds his or her own way to do it. Do not get too upset about their appearance, they will look better cooked—just focus on making them small (about 1 to 2½ inches / 3 to 6 centimeters long). Keep making rolls until you run out of filling.

Line a medium pot well with pieces of leftover cabbage leaves. Place the rolls in the bottom of the pot, arranged snugly in a spiral. Once you've covered the bottom, add a second layer in the same fashion.

Cover the second layer with leftover cabbage leaves, place the bone on top, and cover it all with an inverted plate. Add enough water to nearly reach the plate and cover the pot with a lid. Bring to a boil, then reduce to a simmer and cook for about 1 hour.

The stuffed cabbage leaves are ready when the meat is firm and the cabbage is completely cooked through and soft. Taste one to be sure. Discard the bone and extra cabbage leaves, reserving the cooking liquid for use in the avgolemono.

Make the avgolemono as instructed on page 215; once the sauce is doubled in volume, pour back into the pot with the stuffed cabbage leaves.

Immediately take off the heat and serve in a deep platter with the sauce.

A Simple Green Salad

We use this salad to accompany any shared lunch, dinner, or celebration. The fun part of it is the lettuce, which is cut into very thin strips.

<u>serves</u> • 4 to 6   <u>time</u> • Under 30 minutes

½ cup (125 milliliters) extra-virgin olive oil

2½ tablespoons white wine vinegar

Salt

1 large head romaine lettuce, very thinly sliced horizontally

¼ cup finely chopped scallions (about ½ bunch)

½ cup finely chopped dill (about ½ bunch)

Add the olive oil, vinegar, and salt to a jar. Screw on the lid and shake to combine.

Toss together the lettuce, scallions, and dill in a salad bowl, and then pour the dressing over the top. Toss to coat in the dressing. Taste and adjust the seasoning.

tip

Make some more dressing if the salad seems underdressed to you. This dressing can be made in any quantity by combining 1 part vinegar and 3 parts oil.

Pork with Celeriac

The secret to all stews is to give them time to acquire a depth of flavor. Let them cook on low heat for most of the cooking time, and forget them until you remember with horror that you have forgotten them. Do not overload them with water right from the beginning—add water when necessary, and do lots of other things in between, kitchen related or not.   <u>serves</u> • 4 to 6   <u>time</u> • 4 hours or longer

Extra-virgin olive oil

Salt and pepper

2 pounds (1 kilogram) boneless pork shoulder or collar, cut into 2-inch (5-centimeter) pieces

1 large onion, finely chopped

¾ cup (180 milliliters) white wine

Beef Stock (page 212), Chicken Stock (page 211), or water

3 pounds (1.5 kilograms) celeriac, peeled and cut into 2-inch (5-centimeter) pieces

1 recipe Avgolemono (page 215)

tip

The celeriac in this recipe can be replaced with young celery stalks and leaves (harvested before they grow into thick stalks). These are commonly sold by the bunch in Greece.

Cover the bottom of a large pot with oil and heat over medium high heat. Salt the pork and add it to the pot. Brown on all sides. Remove from the pot and set aside on a plate.

Add the onion to the pot, lower the heat to medium, and cook until translucent. Return the pork to the pot along with the wine. Boil until the alcohol has evaporated. Add water or stock, enough to half-cover the pork. Bring to a boil, cover, then lower to a simmer and cook for 2 hours. Check on it periodically and add water as needed.

Meanwhile, place a large pot of salted water over high heat and bring to a boil. Add the celeriac and boil for 8 to 10 minutes, then drain.

Add the celeriac to the pork and cook for another hour. The celeriac may be fully cooked before the pork; if so, remove it and return it to the pot when the pork is very soft and you still have about 3 ladlefuls of liquid left in the pot. This is the liquid you will use to make your avgolemono.

Make the avgolemono as instructed on page 215. Pour it into the pot with the pork, take hold of both handles, and dance the sauce around the pork until it thickens and reaches a simmer. Take it off the heat and serve immediately.

Beef Stifado

While spending time with Kyria Loula in her own home toward the end of her life, it occurred to me that in all the years she had been an active part of my life and my family, I had never stepped into hers. Even if she was the main provider of the food we ate, her role in our house created an inevitable divide between us, one that wasn't bridged until the moment I showed her that I recognized the vital role she had played throughout my life. I asked her how she came to work in my great-grandmother's kitchen and discovered it was the outcome of a series of serendipitous circumstances: a wedding in the family (my great-uncle Jason's), need for a helping hand in the kitchen, a phone call, and a seamstress (her mother). She told me the story while giving me this recipe.

serves · 6 to 8   time · 4 hours or longer

3 whole cloves

1 large red onion, peeled and left whole

Extra-virgin olive oil

3 pounds (1.5 kilograms) boneless beef chuck or shank, cut into 2-inch (5-centimeter) cubes

1 cup (250 milliliters) red wine

6 medium tomatoes, grated, or one 14-ounce (400-gram) can diced tomatoes

1 juniper berry

2 allspice berries

1/2 orange

Salt and pepper

4 1/2 pounds (2 kilograms) pearl onions or shallots

1/2 cup (125 milliliters) red wine vinegar

1 bay leaf

Stick the cloves into the red onion.

Add 1/2 inch (1 centimeter) olive oil to a large, heavy pot, and place over high heat. Once hot, add the red onion and start browning the beef well on all sides, working in batches. Transfer each batch to a plate as it is browned. When all of the beef is browned, return it to the pot, along with any juices that have accumulated on the plate. Add the wine, and let the alcohol boil off over high heat for 10 minutes, until evaporated.

Add the tomatoes and let boil for 8 minutes. Add the juniper berry, allspice, orange, a generous pinch of salt, pepper, and 2 cups (500 milliliters) of hot water. Reduce the heat to low and let simmer, uncovered.

Meanwhile, prepare the pearl onions: Bring a pot of water to a boil. Add the pearl onions or shallots and boil for 15 minutes. Drain, let cool slightly, then peel. Add a thin layer of olive oil to a frying pan over high heat. Add the peeled onions and cook until they take on some color, stirring occasionally.

Add the pearl onions to the simmering beef mixture and simmer for about 30 minutes, then add the vinegar and 1/4 cup (60 milliliters) of olive oil. Remove the orange.

Continued

tip

You can also make this recipe using rabbit. It is a much more delicate meat than beef, with a subtle taste that turns into a delicious stew.

Continue to simmer the beef mixture for 1½ hours more, then add the bay leaf. Continue to simmer for an hour more, or until the onions are shiny and the meat can be cut into with a fork. Remove the bay leaf and serve with pasta and grated cheese.

Time

*Tomorrow, to exist, needs yesterday
and today,*

an after needs a now and a then

*change presupposes time and the curiosity
to notice the difference*

*cooking fragments time into moments
of change*

and transports into the now of observation

rooting you wherever you are,

*making an unknown place known
to you in seconds*

Yiouvetsi me Hilopites

OVEN-STEWED MEAT WITH EGG PASTA

Yiouvetsi is the name given to stews made in a covered clay oven dish; you can throw anything into it and feel sure that it will come out tasting good. No aromas escape, and the ingredients are never deprived of moisture, as it has no place to go. Yiouvetsi needs plenty of time for the flavors to meld together.

serves • 6 to 8   time • Under 3 hours

3 pounds (1.5 kilograms) boneless beef or lamb chuck or shank, cut into 2-inch (5-centimeter) cubes

Salt and pepper

1½ tablespoons dried oregano

⅓ cup (75 milliliters) extra-virgin olive oil

6 medium tomatoes, grated, or one 14-ounce (400-gram) can diced tomatoes

⅓ cup (80 grams) tomato paste

One 1-pound (500-gram) package hilopites (dried square egg pasta) or orzo

2 tablespoons unsalted butter

3 cups (300 grams) grated kefalotyri or Parmesan cheese

tip

If you don't have a clay dish, you can use a Dutch oven for this recipe.

Preheat the oven to 350°F (180°C).

Season the meat with salt, pepper, and oregano and place in a clay oven dish. Add the olive oil and grated tomatoes. Dilute the tomato paste with ½ cup (125 milliliters) water, then add to the dish and stir well. If needed, add more water so that the liquid half-covers the meat.

Cover with the lid and bake in the oven for 2 to 3 hours. Every now and again check to see if it needs water, topping up with hot water if so.

Meanwhile, cook the pasta in boiling salted water for 5 minutes. Drain well, then add to the meat for the last 20 minutes in the oven. Before adding the pasta, ensure that the liquid in the dish half-covers the meat; if not, add hot water as needed.

When ready, remove from the oven and stir in the butter. The meat should be soft and the pasta tender. Serve with the grated cheese.

Fasolakia me Garides

GREEN BEANS AND SHRIMP

I think this dish encapsulates exactly what my family is—traditional in an earthy way, but refined and cosmopolitan. I am not sure whose recipe this is, but something tells me that it is a recipe Kyria Loula found somewhere and decided to adopt.   serves · 4 to 6   time · Under 2 hours

³/₄ pound (400 grams) medium shrimp in shells with heads and tails intact

¹/₂ tablespoon unsalted butter

Extra-virgin olive oil

1 bay leaf

6 black peppercorns

1 pound (500 grams) green beans

Salt and pepper

1 large white onion, finely chopped

Scant ¹/₂ cup (100 milliliters) white wine

6 tomatoes, grated, or one 14-ounce (400-gram) can diced tomatoes

Scant ¹/₂ cup (100 milliliters) milk

Scant ¹/₂ cup (100 milliliters) crème fraîche or sour cream

1 cup (100 grams) grated Graviera or Gruyère cheese

Peel and devein the shrimp with a toothpick, reserving the heads and shells in a bowl. Melt the butter in a small frying pan over medium to high heat and sauté the shrimp until pink and opaque. Remove from the heat and set aside.

Coat a saucepan with a thin layer of olive oil and add the shrimp shells and heads. Cook over high heat until they turn a nice dark orange color, using a wooden spoon to squash them a few times to release all their flavor. After 8 minutes, add the bay leaf and peppercorns and fill the saucepan with water. Once boiling, reduce the heat to a gentle simmer and allow the shrimp stock to simmer until you are ready to add it to the sauce.

While the stock simmers, clean and cook the green beans: Bring a medium pot of salted water to boil over high heat. Using a vegetable peeler, remove the stringy sides. Use a small knife to cut off the pointy ends, then julienne the beans lengthwise, or let a bean slicer do the work for you. Add the green beans to the boiling water and boil until they have turned a dark green color, but still have a slight crunch to them. Drain well and set aside.

Now take a deep frying pan, coat the bottom with a thin layer of oil and add the onion with a pinch of salt. Cook over medium heat until soft and slightly browned. Add the wine and reduce until the alcohol has evaporated. Add the tomatoes, increase the heat to high, and reduce the mixture for 10 minutes. Holding a sieve over the pan, pour in the simmering shrimp stock (you should have a little over 2 cups / 500 milliliters) and boil vigorously for 2 to 3 minutes. Reduce the heat to medium and allow the sauce to reduce to a quarter of its original volume.

When the sauce is ready, turn the heat down to the lowest setting and add the milk and crème fraîche. Season with salt and pepper. Mix well with a spoon until the sauce is a pale red color, then add the cooked shrimp, reserving a few for garnish.

Sprinkle a large round serving platter with half of the grated cheese, add a third of the beans, and then add a third of the sauce. Repeat the layers, ending with the sauce. Top with the reserved shrimp. Serve warm or cold—either way it's delicious!

You can also layer this dish in a mold for a fancier presentation. Unmold it on a serving platter at room temperature.

The sauce in this recipe can also be used for pasta.

Onion Tart

I made this onion tart for a dinner party. Though I admit it was delicious, I was sad to see that everybody automatically preferred my dish to the host's offering solely because I had been introduced as a chef.

Since I finished cooking school, people assume that I know better than they do when it comes to cooking. While this is true in some cases, I know plenty of grandmas, home cooks, and foodies with no professional training who have a more complex or precise understanding of food than I do. I learn from others as others learn from me.   serves · 4 to 6   time · Under 3 hours

1 Savory Pastry Case (page 218)

Extra-virgin olive oil

2 pounds (1 kilogram) onions, thinly sliced

Salt and pepper

3 large eggs

½ cup (125 milliliters) heavy cream

½ cup (125 milliliters) sour cream or Greek yogurt

¾ cup (80 grams) grated Parmesan or Gruyère cheese

Pinch ground nutmeg

Make the dough for the savory pastry case as instructed on page 218.

Preheat the oven to 350°F (180°C).

While the dough sits in the fridge, heat a drizzle of olive oil in a saucepan over medium low heat. Add the onions and a pinch of salt. Cover and cook for 30 minutes, stirring occasionally, until the onions are soft and caramelized.

While waiting for the onions to caramelize, pre-bake the pastry case as instructed on page 218.

Transfer the caramelized onions to a bowl to cool. Once cool, add the remaining ingredients. Use a fork to mix well, and season to taste.

Pour into the pastry case and bake in the oven for 45 minutes, or until the filling is set. Cool before serving warm or at room temperature.

Pasta au Gratin

This baked pasta is interspersed with caramelized tomatoes that appear as small explosions of sweet flavor within the more subtle flavor of the pasta and béchamel. It has been a staple of many large family gatherings. When cooking for 30 or more guests, not all dishes can be complex; this dish is designed for such occasions.   serves • 6 to 8   time • Under 2 hours

One 1-pound (500-gram)
  package linguine or tagliatelle

Extra-virgin olive oil

6 medium tomatoes, thickly
  sliced

3 tablespoons sugar

Salt and pepper

Butter, for greasing

1/2 cup (60 grams) breadcrumbs

2 cups (200 grams) grated
  Parmesan cheese

béchamel

1 tablespoon unsalted butter

1 tablespoon all-purpose flour

1¼ cups (300 milliliters) milk

2/3 cup (150 milliliters)
  heavy cream

Salt and pepper

Ground nutmeg

tip

You can enrich this dish with various other vegetables, but I suggest you do so only after you have experienced it in its original form.

Cook the pasta in boiling salted water until al dente (cooked but firm). Drain well and drizzle with olive oil to prevent sticking.

Meanwhile, cover the bottom of a large frying pan with olive oil and heat until nearly smoking. Add the tomatoes and sprinkle evenly with the sugar, then season with salt and pepper to taste. Fry for 4 minutes per side, until so soft they may break. Carefully remove from the pan onto a plate and reserve the most beautiful ones to decorate the top of the gratin.

Butter the bottom of a baking dish, then sprinkle with breadcrumbs and about a third of the grated cheese. Add half of the pasta, sprinkle with half of the remaining grated cheese, and top with half the tomatoes. In layers, add the remaining pasta, the remaining grated cheese, and the remaining tomatoes. Drizzle any juices that have accumulated on the plate over the pasta.

Preheat oven to 350°F (180°C).

Make a light béchamel following the method on page 216 with the ingredients listed here. Pour the béchamel over the pasta. Insert a fork at various points and jiggle the dish to distribute the béchamel everywhere.

Bake in the oven for 30 minutes, or until the top starts browning. Make sure the sauce does not completely dry up in the oven, adding a little more cream, if necessary. Serve in the baking dish.

Artichokes à la Polita

This recipe is one of my all-time favorites. It is something I cook for myself and look forward to coming home to eat. Some people hate artichokes, but I cannot imagine why. Not only are they beautiful, their taste is delicate and particular. Even if you are not a fan, teach your children to enjoy them—they will one day be grateful! serves · 4 to 5   time · Under 2 hours

1 tablespoon all-purpose flour

Juice of 2 to 3 lemons

6 artichokes

Extra-virgin olive oil

2 large carrots, cut in pieces

2 potatoes, peeled and cut to the same size as the carrots

4 scallions, finely chopped

1 onion, finely chopped

Salt and pepper

½ cup chopped dill (about ½ bunch)

tip

If you're thinking of buying frozen artichokes for this recipe, do so only if you are really craving them and they are not in season—not out of laziness to clean the fresh ones. Cleaning is part of the process!

Fill a large bowl with water and add the flour and lemon juice. Clean each artichoke by cutting about 1 inch off the top, then breaking off the majority of the hard outer green leaves. Stop once you start seeing very light green leaves. Use a spoon to scoop out the fuzzy choke in the center. To prevent discoloring, place each artichoke in the bowl of lemon juice, flour, and water immediately after cleaning it.

Add a drizzle of olive oil to a medium to large saucepan and heat over medium heat. Add the carrots, potatoes, scallions, onion, and a pinch of salt and cook gently in the oil—don't let them take on any color. Add the artichokes, reserving the water in the bowl, and give them a toss with the vegetables in the pan. Empty the bowl of water, but keep the last part of it that has the flour floating in it, and add it to the pan.

Add more water to just cover the vegetables. Cut a piece of parchment paper to the size of the inside of your pan, oil it, and place directly on top of the vegetables to use as a lid. Bring the mixture to a gentle simmer and cook until the artichokes are fork-tender, about 35 minutes. The sauce should have reduced and thickened. Finish by seasoning to taste and adding the chopped dill. Serve on a platter with feta cheese on the side.

Pita me Lahanika

VEGETABLE PIE

Despite its name, this pie is not actually vegetarian. Meat cunningly found its way in without saying so! This reminds me of two opposing messages I've picked up in the Greek food tradition. Our cuisine produces wonderful, varied dishes for vegetarians, vegans, and omnivores alike, yet gives rise to a population (predominantly the male part) who do not believe they are actually being nourished if a meal does not include meat.   serves • 8 to 10   time • Under 3 hours

Extra-virgin olive oil

1 onion, finely chopped

Salt and pepper

1 pound (500 grams) ground beef

6 tablespoons (90 milliliters) white wine

6 medium tomatoes, grated, or one 14-ounce (400-gram) can diced tomatoes

1 large eggplant, finely diced

1 green bell pepper, finely diced

1 red bell pepper, finely diced

2 small zucchini, finely diced

1 carrot, grated

½ cup chopped parsley leaves (about ½ bunch)

4 large eggs

10 ounces (300 grams) crumbled feta cheese

¾ cup (200 grams) anthotyro or ricotta cheese

1 cup (100 grams) grated Parmesan

One 8-ounce (225-gram) package phyllo dough

1 tablespoon sesame seeds

Coat a large frying pan with a little oil over medium heat. Add the onion with a pinch of salt and cook until soft and translucent. Increase the heat to medium high and add the beef, breaking it up with a wooden spoon. Once it starts browning, add the wine and boil until all the alcohol has evaporated. Add the tomatoes and simmer until thickened and no liquid is left in the pan. Remove from the heat, transfer to a large mixing bowl, and let cool.

Add about 6 tablespoons of olive oil to the same frying pan over medium high heat. Add the eggplant, peppers, zucchini, and carrot and sauté until soft. Transfer to the bowl with the beef mixture and let cool.

Add the parsley and stir in the eggs, one at a time. Finally, add the cheeses and mix well. Season with salt and pepper to taste.

Preheat the oven to 350°F (180°C).

Grease a 13-by-9-inch (33-by-23-centimeter) baking dish or pan with olive oil. Start the pie by laying a phyllo sheet on all four sides of the baking dish. Each sheet should partially cover the bottom of the dish, with the rest hanging over the edge. Brush every piece of phyllo that you lay on the dish with oil. Then place five sheets in the center, brushing each with oil.

Add the filling and cover with five more sheets of phyllo. Cut any excess phyllo away and tuck the phyllo in around the edges of the dish. Brush the top with olive oil, sprinkle with sesame seeds, and bake in the oven for 1 hour, until golden brown.

SUNDAYS

Roast Pork with Apple and Onion

I always felt that going to my cousins' house was special, and I associate this roast with Sunday lunches at their house. Although Kyria Loula cooked nearly the same food there as in my home, there were noticeable differences. I recall her telling me that the taste of her food differed depending on the family for which she was cooking. serves • 6 to 8   time • Under 3 hours

1½ tablespoons salt

1½ tablespoons pepper

1 teaspoon ground cinnamon

2 large cloves garlic

3 to 3½ pounds (1.5 kilograms) fresh ham

3 tablespoons of your favorite mustard

Extra-virgin olive oil

2 tart apples, finely diced

1 large onion, finely chopped

¾ cup (180 milliliters) Beef Stock (page 212), Chicken Stock (page 211), or water

¾ cup (180 milliliters) white wine

3 tablespoons honey

Preheat the oven to 325°F (170°C).

Mix the salt, pepper, and cinnamon in a small bowl. Chop each garlic clove into 3 to 4 pieces.

Lay the pork on a cutting board and rub the area where the bone was with a good amount of the cinnamon mixture and mustard. Cut five holes in the meat and fill each with a little cinnamon mixture, some mustard, and a piece of garlic. Throughout this process there is no need to be tidy—the more the holes overflow with seasoning and mustard the better. Now sew the meat up, securing both sides together with either kitchen string or by passing wooden skewers through both sides of the meat. Rub the outside of the meat with seasoning.

Drizzle a small amount of olive oil into a large frying pan and let it heat up well before you add the pork to brown. Add the pork, but do not rush this process; let each side sit for a while until it really has browned. The better the meat has been seared, the more moisture it will retain while roasting. Once browned on all sides, place in a roasting pan.

Add the apples, onion, and any remaining garlic to the frying pan. Add the stock, white wine, and honey and cook over medium heat, until the apples break easily with the back of a spoon and the sauce has taken on a dark color.

Pour the sauce over the meat, add ¾ cup (180 milliliters) water to the pan, and cover with foil. Roast the pork in the oven for 1½ hours, or until the juices run clear. Five minutes before the end of cooking, remove the foil and raise the oven temperature to 390°F (200°C).

To serve, separate the sauce and the meat; serve the sauce in a sauceboat and the pork on a wooden cutting board. Let the meat sit for 10 minutes and then slice to your preferred thickness (mine is about ½ inch / 1 centimeter thick).

Pork Tenderloin in Mustard Sauce

I hosted a dinner party at a friend's house as a gesture of gratitude and cooked a personal variation of this recipe. I find that cooking is a very genuine way to thank someone. I try to take notice of the time spent and keep my intention in mind the whole time. It is a pure and simple gesture, and people are always more excited to eat something you've made yourself than any premade option, irrespective of the degree of difficulty you have gone through to make it.

serves • 4 to 6   time • Under 2 hours

Extra-virgin olive oil

2 pork tenderloins

1 large white onion, finely chopped

¾ cup (180 milliliters) white wine

1 cup plus 2 tablespoons (275 milliliters) Beef Stock (page 212), Chicken Stock (page 211), or water

¾ cup (180 milliliters) heavy cream

2 tablespoons Dijon mustard, or your favorite kind

¾ cup (75 grams) grated Parmesan cheese

Salt and pepper

tip

Be careful to not overcook the meat at any stage. Keep an eye on it at all times!

Preheat the oven to 350°F (180°C).

Place a frying pan over high heat. Once hot, add a thin layer of olive oil. Add the pork and brown well on all sides. Remove from the heat and set aside.

Add the onion to the pan and cook until translucent. Pour in the white wine and let it boil until the alcohol has evaporated. Add the stock and reduce to half its original volume. Add the cream and mustard and simmer for 5 minutes, until the sauce thickens slightly. Taste, adding more cream if too mustardy or more mustard if too bland, then remove the pan from the heat. Add the grated cheese and season with salt and pepper. Taste again, and adjust the mustard, the cheese, and the seasoning, if needed.

Place the pork loin directly on the oven rack, with a pan beneath it to collect drippings. Roast in the oven for 8 minutes. Remove and let rest for 5 minutes.

Slice the pork loin into pieces about ¾ inch (1.5 centimeters) thick, and add any remaining juices to the mustard sauce. The meat should be a rosy pink color in the center. Lay the pork slices on the bottom of a deep baking dish, and then pour the sauce over the top.

Bake in the oven for 10 minutes and no more! Serve in the baking dish or on a beautiful large platter.

Three Purées Worth Mastering

The following three purée recipes will provide you with more than enough knowledge to make a purée out of anything you wish, but before you go on to making things new, you must first master the basics, dissect them, and extract from them all they have to teach. Perhaps this can be applied to all areas of life— to create something new, you need to know where you are starting from and what preceded you.

Spinach Purée

serves · 4 to 6   time · Under 1 hour

2 pounds (1 kilogram) spinach, washed, stems removed

1 tablespoon unsalted butter

1 onion, chopped

béchamel

1½ tablespoons unsalted butter

1½ tablespoons all-purpose flour

1½ cups (350 milliliters) milk

3 tablespoons heavy cream

Salt and pepper

Ground nutmeg

1½ cups (150 grams) grated Parmesan cheese

Add about ½ inch (1 centimeter) of water and the spinach to a large pot over medium heat and cover with a lid. Let the spinach wilt, checking periodically to stir and ensure nothing is stuck to the bottom of the pot.

Meanwhile, add the butter to a deep frying pan over medium heat. Add the onion and cook until translucent. Once the spinach has wilted, drain off any excess water and add the spinach to the onion. Cook for about 5 minutes, then transfer to a food processor or blender.

Make the béchamel following the method on page 216 and using the ingredients listed here. Add the béchamel to the spinach mixture, then process until smooth but slightly textured. Add the grated cheese and season with salt and pepper to taste. If the mixture is too thick or dark, add some cream or milk.

Transfer the purée back to the pot used to cook the spinach and reheat, but do not boil. Serve immediately to accompany just about anything!

Potato Purée

serves • 4 to 6   time • Under 1 hour

5 large potatoes (about
   3 pounds / 1.5 kilograms)

Salt and pepper

2 cups (500 milliliters) milk

⅓ cup (75 milliliters) heavy
   cream

Handful grated cheese of
   your choice

1 tablespoon unsalted butter

Ground nutmeg

Place the whole, unpeeled potatoes in a large pot of salted water. Cover and bring to a boil, then reduce the heat and simmer until very soft. Drain well.

Heat the milk and cream together in a small pan. Keep hot.

When they are cool enough to handle, peel the potatoes and return to the pot. Using a hand mixer, start mixing the potatoes into a mash, then add the hot milk and cream. Keep mixing until a smooth purée is achieved, and add more milk or cream if the mixture needs thinning. Add the grated cheese and butter and mix with a spoon, then season with salt, pepper, and nutmeg to taste.

The texture should be smooth and almost elastic. You can make your purée as smooth or as textured as you wish. It depends on what you are going to do with it. If you want to nestle a poached egg in it, make it rough and chunky; if you want to lay a few small Soutzoukakia (page 32) over it, make it smooth.

Carrot Purée

serves • 4 to 6   time • Under 1 hour

9 large carrots (about 2 pounds /
1 kilogram), peeled

1 medium potato

¼ cup (60 milliliters) sour cream
or Greek yogurt

Salt and white pepper

tip

*Add an onion to the
carrots and potato while
boiling, then blend with about
2 cups (500 milliliters) of
the cooking liquid to make a
delicious soup!*

Boil the carrots and the unpeeled potato in a large pot
of salted water. Once a fork can easily cut through
them, drain well. When cool enough to handle, peel
the potato, then place the potato and carrots in a food
processor or blender and purée until smooth.

Return the carrot and potato purée to the pot and
add the sour cream, salt, and white pepper. Bring to a
gentle simmer and stir until thickened to your liking.
Serve hot.

Enjoy with Kotopoulo sto Fourno (page 70), or a
fried egg and some cheese.

Spinach Gnocchi

When I made the first list of recipes to be included in this cookbook, this one did not cross my mind as it is more like a Greek adaptation of a traditional Italian recipe, but as it was a personal favorite of Kyria Loula, who thought it vital to be included, I cannot but obey her wish. After having cooked it on multiple occasions to feed large groups, I think I realize what made it one of Kyria Loula's favorites: *everybody* falls in love with it!   serves • 3 to 4   time • Under 2 hours

1⅓ pounds (600 grams) spinach, washed, stems removed

Extra-virgin olive oil

½ onion, finely chopped

Salt and pepper

Ground nutmeg

1 large egg

5 ounces (150 grams) crumbled feta cheese

¾ cup (150 grams) anthotyro or ricotta cheese

1 cup (125 grams) all-purpose flour

⅓ cup (30 grams) grated Parmesan cheese

4½ ounces (120 grams) Gorgonzola or other blue cheese

1 scant cup (100 milliliters) heavy cream

1 scant cup (100 milliliters) milk

Put about ½ inch (1 centimeter) of water and the spinach in a large pot over medium heat and cover with a lid. Let the spinach wilt, then take the lid off and cook until all the water has evaporated. Place the spinach in a fine-mesh sieve and squeeze dry.

Coat the same pot with a thin layer of olive oil over medium heat. Once hot add the onion and cook until translucent. Add the spinach and cook for 5 minutes. Season with some pepper and nutmeg, place back in the sieve, and allow to cool.

Beat the egg in a medium bowl, then add the feta and anthotyro cheeses and cooled spinach and onion. Combine until the mixture turns into a lumpy dough, and then season to taste with salt, pepper, and nutmeg.

Fill a large pot three-quarters full of salted water and bring to a boil.

While waiting for the water to boil, make the gnocchi: Lay out a piece of parchment paper on your work surface and add the flour in a mound to one side of the sheet. Take small pieces of dough and shape them into oval balls about ¾ inch (1.5 centimeters) long. Roll them carefully in the flour and arrange them neatly on the empty side of the sheet.

Add the gnocchi to the boiling water, cooking 10 pieces at a time. They will sink to the bottom when placed in the water, but will rise to the top once they're cooked. When they begin floating, remove them with a slotted spoon and place in a buttered baking dish, arranged in neat rows. Sprinkle with grated Parmesan.

Preheat the oven to 350°F (180°C).

Combine the Gorgonzola, cream, and milk in a saucepan over medium heat. Bring it to a boil, then reduce the heat and simmer for 10 minutes. Season to taste with pepper and nutmeg. Pour over the gnocchi.

Bake in the oven for 15 to 20 minutes, until the sauce starts turning a golden color and thickens slightly.

Butternut Squash Soup

I love making soups. I believe they are a great place to start a meal, or a great meal in and of themselves. Here is a recipe that uses the basic French velouté technique I learned at cooking school in Spain, right in the middle of a Greek family cookbook. It is a recipe of my own in my family's cookbook; a seed I am planting in the middle of the past, to grow into a runway for the future. serves • 4 to 6   time • Under 2 hours

Extra-virgin olive oil

1 onion, chopped

1 leek, chopped

1 carrot, chopped

1 clove garlic, crushed

Salt and pepper

1 bay leaf

Pinch ground cinnamon

2 pounds (1 kilogram) butternut squash, peeled and cut into 2-inch (5-centimeter) pieces

1 teaspoon almond extract

Add a thin layer of olive oil to a large pot over medium heat. Add the onion, leek, carrot, garlic, a big pinch of salt, the bay leaf, and cinnamon. Cook, covered, until the vegetables start taking on color.

Add the squash and ½ cup (125 milliliters) of water, cover, and cook until the squash is so soft it is mushy, 20 to 25 minutes. If it starts to stick to the bottom of the pot at any point, add a little more water and lower the heat.

Take off the heat and cool slightly. Remove the bay leaf. Pour the mixture into a blender or use an immersion blender to purée until totally smooth.

Pour the soup back into the pot and season with salt and pepper to taste. Add the almond extract and extra water if the soup is too thick. Reheat until just simmering, then serve.

Apple Soufflé

I remember this dessert as something that Kyria Loula made. My cousin Amalia remembers it as a dessert that her mum used to make. Someone else from my family may have another memory. Irrespective of memories and stories, this dessert is unusual and easy. The apples cook in the oven until soft and caramelized, the soufflé topping is buttery and smooth and looks absolutely beautiful until you cut into it; then it becomes a delicious baked apple and batter mess.

serves • 6 to 8   time • Under 3 hours

4½ pounds (2 kilograms) tart apples, peeled, cored, and thinly sliced

⅓ cup (70 grams) brown sugar

2 teaspoons ground cinnamon

2½ tablespoons unsalted butter

soufflé mixture

1½ cups (190 grams) all-purpose flour

1 teaspoon baking powder

1 teaspoon ground cinnamon

¾ cup (1½ sticks / 170 grams) unsalted butter, room temperature

¾ cup (150 grams) granulated sugar

3 large eggs, separated

1 teaspoon vanilla extract

Powdered sugar, for serving

Preheat the oven to 375°F (190°C). Butter a large soufflé or gratin dish. Layer the sliced apples in the prepared dish, sprinkling evenly with the brown sugar and 2 teaspoons cinnamon. Finish with 2½ tablespoons butter dotted around the apples in small pieces.

Bake in the oven, stirring every so often, for about 1 hour, or until the apples soften and take on a beautiful dark brown color. Remove the apples from the oven and set aside to cool.

In the meantime, make the soufflé mixture: Sift together the flour, baking powder, and 1 teaspoon cinnamon and set aside.

Beat the ¾ cup butter, granulated sugar, egg yolks, and vanilla together until light and creamy, using an electric mixer. In a separate bowl, beat the egg whites to stiff peaks.

Alternately fold the flour mixture and the egg whites into the butter mixture. Using a spatula, scrape the sides of the mixing bowl and tip the bowl over the baking dish with the apples to allow the mixture to fall over the apples, covering them completely.

Bake in the oven for 20 minutes, then turn off the oven and let it sit in the oven for another 20 minutes. Before serving, sprinkle with powdered sugar and serve with whipped cream or custard on the side.

Cooked Uncooked Chocolate Cake

This recipe is the cause of much enthusiasm in my family. It's dedicated to the chocolate lovers—the children and adults—who have trembled, giggled, and anticipated with excitement the oozing texture of this not-too-sweet chocolate cake. I wish I could include a recording of my cousin Sofia describing this cake. It would make you want to bake and eat it now.

serves • 8 to 10   time • Under 1 hour

9 ounces (250 grams) bittersweet chocolate, chopped

8 large eggs, separated

1 cup (200 grams) granulated sugar

1 cup (2 sticks) plus 2 tablespoons (250 grams) unsalted butter, diced, room temperature

1²/₃ cups (200 grams) all-purpose flour

1 teaspoon baking powder

Zest of 1 orange

1 teaspoon vanilla extract

3 tablespoons brandy

Preheat the oven to 375°F (190°C). Grease a 9-inch (23-centimeter) round springform cake pan and dust with flour, shaking out the excess.

Melt the chocolate in a double boiler or carefully in a small saucepan, stirring constantly until it melts. Remove from the heat.

Beat the egg yolks and the sugar until pale and fluffy. Add the butter and the melted chocolate and beat well. Fold in the flour, baking powder, orange zest, vanilla, and brandy with a spatula.

Beat the egg whites to stiff peaks. Gently fold into the cake mixture. Tip the mixture into the prepared pan.

Bake the cake in the oven for 15 minutes. (Shake it to see if the center is wobbly.) Remove from the oven immediately and let sit for 10 minutes. Keep in mind that the center is so soft you will need both a spoon and a spatula to serve. You can leave it in the oven longer, but that means you will have a fully cooked chocolate cake, not the half-cooked one you are looking to make here. Remove the ring of the pan and serve warm with cold cream.

Aunt Eleni's Galaktoboureko

To my great-aunt, this is my great-great-aunt Eleni's recipe; to my mum, it belongs to my great-aunt; and to everyone in my family, it is the best galaktoboureko we have ever eaten. We make galaktoboureko once a year for Easter Sunday. It differs slightly from the traditional classic in that our recipe has toasted almonds, and it also has more eggs in the cream. Until I was given the recipe, my great-aunt was the only one who made it. Now, I am proud to say, it has been collectively decided within the family that mine is as good as hers, or perhaps even better.   serves • 8 to 12   time • Under 3 hours

2²/₃ cups (625 milliliters) milk

¹/₃ cup (60 grams) fine semolina

1²/₃ cups plus 6 tablespoons (410 grams) granulated sugar

1 wide strip orange zest, plus finely grated zest of 1 orange

5 tablespoons cold butter, plus about 5 tablespoons melted butter for brushing

Juice of ¹/₂ orange

4 large eggs

²/₃ cup (100 grams) finely chopped almonds, toasted

One 8-ounce (225-gram) package phyllo dough

Put the milk in a pot over medium heat. Once warm, add the semolina. Stir with a wooden spoon, pausing every so often to allow the mixture to start simmering gently. As time passes you will feel it thickening, and at this point add 6 tablespoons sugar and the strip of orange zest. The mixture is ready when it becomes so thick that it's hard to stir, 25 to 30 minutes.

Remove the pot from the heat and remove the piece of orange zest. Stir in the 5 tablespoons cold butter, the orange juice, and grated zest. Lightly beat the eggs in a bowl and add to the mixture once it has cooled.

Preheat the oven to 350°F (180°C).

Now you are ready to start assembling the galaktoboureko. Start by brushing a glass or metal 13-by-9-inch (33-by-23-centimeter) baking pan with some of the melted butter and sprinkling with a bit of the almonds. Lay a sheet of phyllo over the almonds, brush with 3 tablespoons melted butter, and sprinkle with enough almonds to create a thin, sparse layer of them. Repeat with half of the remaining phyllo sheets and almonds, then top with the semolina cream. Top the cream with a sheet of phyllo, brush with butter, and sprinkle with almonds. Repeat until all the phyllo has been used. Seal together any pastry that's hanging over the pan by twisting together the edges. Score the top layer, marking the pieces that you'll cut later.

Bake in the oven for 1½ hours, until the phyllo is a dark golden brown. Remove from the oven and let cool completely.

Once cool, prepare the syrup: Combine ⅔ cup (160 milliliters) water and the remaining 1⅔ cups sugar in a small pan and bring to a boil over medium heat, then lower the heat and simmer for 5 to 7 minutes. The syrup is ready when it falls like a ribbon off the spoon.

Pour half of the hot syrup over the cooled galaktoboureko. Immediately cut through the scored pieces you made earlier, cutting all the way through to the bottom, then pour the remaining syrup over the pieces. Allow the syrup to soak in and cool completely before serving.

If you feel there's too much syrup, reserve whatever remains in a jar in the fridge to sweeten a cold coffee or for when you make Baklava (page 171).

Summer Holidays

My family, along with friends who popped in and out of our life for lunch or dinner, is at the core of my summer memories. Summer was a noisy and joyful time of unhampered exposure to the elements.

In the summer, people celebrate in an abstract way. Nature offers us abundant fruits and vegetables, and it is a time of year when everything is elaborately simple. Summer food reflects just this; tables overflow with small plates of food showing off the inherent qualities of each ingredient. But it is also about slow enjoyment, like savoring the taste of a piece of octopus, and hoping the memory lasts until the next time you can eat it, whether that is in a few days or a whole year away.

The majority of the dishes you will find in this chapter can be made in advance, kept in the fridge for quite a few days, and served for an impromptu occasion. If you take a liking to these recipes, I suggest you stock up on the basic ingredients so that you are ready to make them when the need arises. Few require strange or odd ingredients and if you have a vegetable garden, you will notice that all the recipes will make good use of your homegrown produce.

Kaiki Tuna Salad

I wanted to name this recipe "Daddy's Tuna Salad" because it is his recipe, but when I received it from him, he had already given it a title. As is consistent with my father's humble and discreet demeanor, he gave ownership of it to his old Greek wooden boat (*kaiki*), an extension of himself.

This dish, like no other, has the power to bring my father and the things I feel for him alive. It holds within it his movement, taste, voice, and personality—so, apart from the fantastic taste, this is why I love it!

serves • 4 to 5   time • Under 1 hour

dressing

1 small onion, finely chopped

5 tablespoons capers

2 tablespoons mayonnaise

1 tablespoon Dijon mustard

2 teaspoons red wine vinegar or lemon juice

1½ teaspoons ketchup

1 teaspoon extra-virgin olive oil

Dash Worcestershire sauce

Pinch sugar

Salt and pepper

Two 5-ounce (142-gram) cans tuna in oil or water, drained

2 tomatoes, sliced

Chopped fresh basil, to garnish

Make the dressing: Combine all of the dressing ingredients in a jar. Cover with a lid and shake vigorously. The dressing should be relatively thick.

Place the tuna in a bowl and break the large chunks into smaller pieces with a fork. Pour the dressing over the tuna and mix well, but gently, to avoid making the mixture mushy. Let the mixture sit in the fridge for about 30 minutes before serving.

Serve as a meze. Arrange the tomato slices on a serving plate. Drain off any excess liquid from the tuna salad, then spoon it over the tomato slices and sprinkle with chopped basil. Serve with a loaf of fresh bread.

tip

It is easy to make this dish any time of year (though I grew up eating it in the summer) as it doesn't require any special ingredients, and all the ingredients have a long shelf life.

Salata me Mavromatika

BLACK-EYED PEA SALAD

This black-eyed pea salad is one of many cold boiled legume salad variations we make in Greece. You can substitute lentils, chickpeas, or small white beans for the black-eyed peas, and add all sorts of chopped vegetables to make the salad more or less intricate. Make sure to stock your pantry with a variety of dried beans to have the seed of a healthy meal on hand any time.

serves • 4 to 6   time • Under 2 hours

One 16-ounce (500-gram) package dried black-eyed peas

Salt and pepper

4 scallions, finely chopped

2 tomatoes, seeded and chopped

1/2 cup finely chopped parsley leaves (about 1/2 bunch)

2/3 cup (150 milliliters) extra-virgin olive oil

3 1/2 tablespoons white wine vinegar

7 ounces (200 grams) crumbled feta cheese

Boil the peas in salted water for 5 to 8 minutes, or until the water has turned a dark gray color. Drain well, then add the peas back to the pot with fresh water to cover. Bring to a boil, add salt, and simmer until the peas are soft.

Drain the peas and place in a bowl. Chill in the fridge for 30 minutes. Once cool, add the scallions, tomatoes, parsley (reserve a bit for garnish), olive oil, vinegar, and pepper to taste. Mix well, and sprinkle the crumbled feta over the top. Taste a forkful with some feta, and then adjust the seasoning if necessary. Sprinkle with the reserved parsley and serve in a salad bowl.

Tyropitakia

MINI CHEESE PIES

When you make the decision to train professionally as a cook, people assume you have spent your childhood in the kitchen cooking or interested in food. It didn't really happen like this for me. Growing up, I was mostly interested in eating, but I do remember making these small triangular cheese pies as a summer meze. <u>makes</u> • 48 pieces   <u>time</u> • Under 2 hours

béchamel

¾ cup (95 grams) all-purpose flour

7 tablespoons (100 grams) unsalted butter

2 cups (500 milliliters) milk

3 tablespoons heavy cream

Salt and pepper

Ground nutmeg

5 large eggs

18 ounces (500 grams) crumbled feta cheese

1 cup (250 grams) anthotyro or ricotta cheese

1¾ cups (250 grams) grated regato or Gruyère cheese

Salt and pepper

One 16-ounce (450-gram) package phyllo dough

Extra-virgin olive oil

Make the béchamel as directed on page 216 and using the ingredients listed here. Transfer to a bowl to cool.

Combine the cooled béchamel with the eggs, adding one at a time and beating between each addition. Add the cheeses and season to taste.

Preheat the oven to 350°F (180°C).

Place two phyllo sheets on top of each other and cut them into vertical strips 2 inches (5 centimeters) wide. Place a teaspoon of filling near the bottom right corner of each narrow strip of the phyllo, and brush the rest of the strip with olive oil. Fold the bottom left corner of phyllo diagonally over the filling to form a triangular shape. Continue folding the strip, alternating between the left and right sides and maintaining a triangular shape, until you reach the end of the piece of phyllo. Brush the outer edge with milk or water to seal.

Line two baking sheets with parchment paper and arrange the triangular cheese pies neatly in rows.

Bake in the oven until the phyllo is golden brown, 30 to 40 minutes.

tip

To make a whole cheese pie, lay the phyllo as instructed on page 34 and bake it in a 13-by-9-inch (33-by-23-centimeter) baking dish or metal baking tin.

Greek Salad

To me this salad epitomizes the value of eating in season and being close to the source of your food. To fail to do either of the above is to fall short of achieving this salad's full potential. You will have to be patient, selective in the ingredients you pick, and conscientious.   serves • 4 to 5   time • Under 30 minutes

5 ripe tomatoes, cut into irregular pieces

1 small onion, thinly sliced in half moons

Sea salt

7 ounces (200 grams) crumbled feta or mizithra cheese

6 tablespoons extra-virgin olive oil

Mix all the ingredients in a bowl in the order in which they are written, adjusting for taste as needed. Serve with a loaf of fresh bread to dip into any remaining olive oil and juices of the tomato at the end.

Tyrokafteri

SPICY CHEESE DIP

There is something self-assuring about mastering the cuisine you grew up eating. You no longer need others to provide you with the tastes of your past; now you can provide them for yourself and share them with others. I generally tend to use much less oil than the majority of Greek cooks, but when testing the recipes for this book, I realized that sometimes the extra oil is necessary to give the dish its authentic taste. Here, the oil gives the dip its lightness and keeps it from being overly cheesy.

makes • 2 cups   time • Under 30 minutes

2 green chiles, seeds removed

⅓ cup (75 milliliters) extra-virgin olive oil

7 ounces (200 grams) feta cheese

7 ounces (200 grams) anthotyro or ricotta cheese

½ cup (100 grams) Greek yogurt or sour cream

2 tablespoons white wine vinegar

1 small garlic clove, or more to taste

Fry the chiles in the oil over medium to low heat until they are soft. Let cool.

Put the fried chiles and all the remaining ingredients in a food processor and blend together, leaving the dip slightly chunky for a heartier experience when eating it.

Accompany with bread, fried potatoes, Keftedakia (page 151), or Arakas (page 64) or spread on a slice of bread. It will last in the fridge for up to 5 days.

tip

Adjust the chiles and garlic in this recipe to your liking. Keep in mind that as written it is medium to low on the spicy scale, and be careful with the garlic, as excessive garlic can render this dip impossible to eat.

Octopus Marinated in Vinegar

If I could eat the sea, grilled octopus is what I imagine it would taste like. I know that not all of you have access to a charcoal grill or hours of sun to dry the octopus before grilling, so this recipe is the best possible alternative to a grilled octopus served in an idyllic setting near the sea.

serves • 6 to 8   time • Under 3 hours

1 whole octopus, about
  3 pounds (1.5 kilograms)

2 bay leaves

10 black peppercorns

About 1 cup (250 milliliters)
  extra-virgin olive oil

About ½ cup (125 milliliters)
  white wine vinegar

Dried oregano (optional)

Wash the octopus well and remove the eyes and the beak, if it has not already been done. Add about ½ inch (1 centimeter) of water to a large saucepan, and add the whole octopus, bay leaves, and peppercorns. Bring to a boil, cover, then reduce the heat and simmer until tender (a knife should be able to cut through the octopus without much effort). Start checking after about 30 minutes. The more you cook it the softer it becomes; you want it to be soft, not mushy. Once ready, take off the heat and cool in the pan.

Once cool, drain and cut the octopus into bite-size pieces and place in a nonmetallic bowl. Cover with the olive oil and vinegar, and let it marinate in the fridge for at least 1½ hours. Taste and adjust seasoning and sprinkle with oregano, if using, before serving.

✳ ✳ ✳

Fava

YELLOW SPLIT PEA PURÉE

I have this strange affliction: if someone I care for loves eating something, I want to be able to share in his or her joy. This desire becomes stronger the more affection I have for a person. This happened with the feta I saw my father eating chunks of while I was growing up; the bread, butter, and jam a beloved friend of mine ate for breakfast with appetite; and quite a few other things, including fava.

I was not drawn to fava at a young age. It was only much later that I noticed that whenever I shared a meal with friends or family on lazy summer afternoons or late-night dinners, fava seemed to always appear on the table. I finally decided I must experience it and—unlike melon, which I try and try to like but simply cannot—fava soon started giving me pleasure. I am grateful for this flexibility of taste, as I have learned to enjoy foods that, on my own, I may never have discovered.   serves • 6 to 8   time • Under 2 hours

2 cups (400 grams) yellow split peas

¼ cup (60 milliliters) extra-virgin olive oil, plus more for pot

1 medium onion, puréed or finely chopped

Salt and pepper

Start by boiling a large pot full of water. Add the split peas and boil for 2 to 3 minutes, then drain and wipe the pot clean.

Cover the bottom of the pot with oil and place over medium high heat. Add the onion and cook until nearly colored. Add the split peas and cook with the onion for a minute, stirring to coat them in the oil. Add water to cover. Bring to a boil, covered, then reduce to a simmer and cook for about an hour. While cooking, listen to whether the peas ask for more water—make sure that the mixture remains moist but doesn't have excess water.

The fava is ready when it starts dissolving and turning to mush. Using an immersion blender, purée it to your desired consistency—leave it smooth or chunky, depending on how you have envisioned it. Season with salt and pepper and mix in ¼ cup (60 milliliters) olive oil with a spoon.

Serve as a meze with thinly chopped fresh onions, a drizzle of olive oil, capers, thinly sliced radish, caramelized onions, and/or Octopus Marinated in Vinegar (page 139).

Gavros Marinatos

MARINATED ANCHOVIES

When I visited Kyria Loula to collect the recipes for this book, even in the pain of age and illness, she cooked me the dishes she knew I liked to eat. One of them is this meze. In my opinion, Kyria Loula's gavros marinatos puts most others to shame. Unfortunately, she had mastered it to such an extent that when she gave me the recipe, she didn't think it was necessary to give me specific quantities or an exact procedure. I tested the recipe again and again, until I replicated the taste I remember, so that you can make and enjoy it as much as I have in the past.

serves • 6 to 8   time • Under 8 hours

1 pound (500 grams) fresh anchovies

Juice of 3 lemons

2 tablespoons sea salt

1 small clove garlic, slivered

Pepper

Extra-virgin olive oil

tip

Once you have mastered this recipe, and if you are feeling creative, you can use the same procedure with other small fish, like sardines, and play around with the addition of Mediterranean herbs.

Clean the anchovies with your fingers. Scoop out the intestines, pinch off the head, and pull out the spine. Pull off the top fins gently. The only connecting point between the two fillets should be the tail. Wash them well under running water.

Neatly place a layer of anchovies skin side down in a plastic or glass container with a lid. Cover the first layer with abundant lemon juice and sprinkle evenly with salt. Repeat the layers until all the anchovies have been added. Pour over the remaining lemon juice and let marinate for a minimum of 6 hours in the fridge.

Drain the anchovies and place back into the container. Add the garlic and pepper, then cover with olive oil. Covered in oil, the anchovies will keep for 10 days in the fridge. They can be enjoyed as a meze or a snack, or added to a pasta dish or a salad.

Greek Food Simplicity

Simple can be a derogatory adjective or a glorious attribute. I like to think that simple food can breed simple people with simple thoughts and unassuming words. People who would mimic the essence of a boiled vegetable or a grilled fish with nothing to spice it up but some salt and olive oil if need be. And interact just like they do with the salt and the oil, as separate entities unafraid to show their un-obtruded truth.

In places and at times when food cannot be taken for granted I imagine that there is a magic to that which nourishes not because of taste or appearance but because of the basic quality of being able to sustain a human life. And I assume that this revelation of the essential makes those who live it relate in a different way to that around them, with appreciation and humility. Their intellect blunted and senses alert—not because of incapability but because of priority. There is no room for lazy consumption of the complicated and the simple, without knowing the difference, when you are trying to survive.

But through our imagination we can appreciate the complicated like one who eats simply, and feast like one who has never feasted. And reality offers the opportunity to cook and eat, both the simple and the complicated, all within the sphere of choice.

Dolmadakia

STUFFED GRAPE LEAVES

Kyria Loula always made our dolmadakia. They were tightly rolled, tiny, and tasty. Toward the final years of her life, when she had slowly withdrawn from her cooking responsibilities, she would sit patiently in her home and make them for my mother. Cooking gave Kyria Loula a raison d'être. It was the time she managed to give to others but also to herself. I believe being a good cook requires acceptance of one's self, even if just for the time spent in the kitchen. Unconsciously or not, when cooking for others, every cook must view themselves as an integral part of a process, and accept their ability to contribute positively to the outcome.

makes • 60 pieces   time • Under 3 hours

Extra-virgin olive oil

1 large onion, grated

2 cups (300 grams) uncooked white rice

½ cup (60 grams) pine nuts, toasted

½ cup (70 grams) golden raisins

½ cup finely chopped dill (about ½ bunch)

⅓ cup finely chopped mint (about ½ bunch)

Salt and pepper

80 grape leaves

1 cup (200 grams) Greek yogurt

tip

You can use grape leaves from a jar, or if you find them fresh, simply submerge them in boiling water for a few minutes, then drain and let cool before stuffing.

Heat a generous drizzle of olive oil in a frying pan, add the onion, and cook until soft and translucent. Transfer to a large mixing bowl and add the rice, pine nuts, golden raisins, and herbs. Stir until everything is evenly dispersed. Season with salt and pepper and stir in 2 tablespoons of olive oil.

Lay a grape leaf, smooth side down, on a cutting board and cut off any thick stems. Put ½ tablespoon of filling at the base, fold over, tuck in the sides, then roll up all the way. Avoid rolling too tightly, as the rice will expand while cooking. Repeat with the remaining grape leaves and filling.

Line the bottom of a large pot with grape leaves. Add the dolmadakia to the pot in a single layer, fitting them snugly into the pot in a spiral. Continue adding spiraling layers until all the dolmadakia have been added. Season with salt, add a drizzle of olive oil, and cover with a plate. Add water to the pot until the dolmadakia, but not the plate, are covered. Partially cover the pan with a lid, and simmer over medium low heat for 40 to 45 minutes, adding water as needed to keep the dolmadakia from burning. Check for doneness and remove from the heat when the rice is cooked and the water has mostly evaporated. Serve on small plates with a dollop of yogurt on the side.

Melitzanosalata

ROASTED EGGPLANT DIP

While I have altered some recipes in this book to reflect my personal preferences, I give you this recipe exactly as it was given to me—such praise has this melitzanosalata received, it would be almost sinful to do otherwise. It's so good as is, I promise that it will convince even those who think they despise eggplants to love it! Burn the outside of the fresh eggplants very well, leaving them with a hardened, charred outer layer and a juicy inside.

makes • 3 cups   time • Under 2 hours

3 large eggplants

1 large egg yolk

1 tablespoon soy sauce

A few drops Tabasco

2 tablespoons Mayonnaise (page 214)

2 tablespoons extra-virgin olive oil

Salt and pepper

Start by roasting the eggplants. You can do this in the oven under the broiler, over a flame on a gas stove, or the way I do it—in an old frying pan without any oil. Stab the skin a few times before you start, to prevent the eggplants from exploding. Blacken the eggplants on all sides, leaving each side to char for longer than you would expect. Once blackened on all sides, plunge the eggplants into cold water, then drain.

Scoop out the flesh of the eggplants and place in a bowl, trying to avoid most of the skin (do not worry if there is some, it will just add to the taste!). Remove the seeds only if there are many—keep in mind that eggplants have more seeds toward the end of their season.

Discard any excess liquid from the eggplants that has collected in the bowl. Transfer the flesh to a food processor or blender along with the remaining ingredients. Pulse to combine to a smooth texture (like my family makes it) or leave it a little more textured (as I make it in my house). Taste and adjust the seasoning.

Keftedakia
MINI MEATBALLS

The title gives a critical clue as to the greatness of these meatballs: they are so small you can pop them in your mouth whole. If not served as a meze, they can be served with fried potatoes and feta cheese. If you feel like cooking up a feast, accompany them with Fasolakia Ladera (page 53) and add a freshly cut tomato salad for some rawness.

serves • 8 to 10 as a meze, 4 to 6 as a main   time • Under 2 hours

5 slices stale thin sandwich bread, crusts removed and slices soaked in water

1 onion, cut into large pieces

1 pound (500 grams) ground beef

⅓ pound (150 grams) ground pork

1 large egg

2 tablespoons extra-virgin olive oil

2 tablespoons red wine vinegar

½ cup finely chopped parsley leaves (about ½ bunch)

Chopped fresh mint, to taste (optional)

Salt and pepper

All-purpose flour, for rolling

Sunflower or corn oil, for frying

Squeeze the bread well to remove as much water as you can. Mince it with the onion in a food processor, then transfer to a large mixing bowl with the remaining meatball ingredients. Knead together until well combined. Taste to check the seasoning and adjust if needed. (You may brown a small ball of the meat mixture in a frying pan first if you prefer not to taste it raw.)

Form small balls of about 1 inch (2 centimeters) if you want to serve them as a meze, or 2 inches (5 centimeters) if you want to eat them as a main course. Roll them in flour.

Add about ½ inch (1 centimeter) of sunflower oil to a large frying pan and heat over medium high heat. Add the meatballs, cook on all sides until browned (about 6 minutes per batch), then drain on paper towels. Avoid overcrowding the pan—it will lower the temperature substantially and slow the process down.

Serve on small plates or bowls if serving as a meze, or on a large plate for a main meal.

Taramosalata

COD ROE DIP

What stood out to me most in the process of composing this book is the way people embraced the opportunity to talk about the food they enjoyed while growing up and the food they cook for their children. The universality contained in our unique experiences has given me reason to believe that the process I have gone through to make this book may prove to be valuable for all.

makes • About 2½ cups   time • Under 30 minutes

1 small onion, cut into large pieces

2 slices bread, crusts removed and slices soaked in water

Scant ½ cup (100 grams) cod roe

¾ cup (180 milliliters) sunflower oil

½ cup (120 milliliters) extra-virgin olive oil

⅓ cup (75 milliliters) lemon juice

Purée the onion to a pulp in a food processor or blender. Squeeze excess water out of the bread and add it to the onion along with the roe. Start blending. Once well combined, start adding the sunflower oil in a thin stream. You will notice that as the oil is incorporated, the mixture will become thick and smooth. Keep adding oil until the mixture has doubled in volume.

While still blending, add the olive oil and the lemon juice. Taste and add more lemon juice if it is too fishy for your liking. Keep adding a little lemon juice at a time until you are happy with it. If it is the first time you are trying this recipe and have no point of comparison, just make it taste good—like something you would love to dip a large piece of fresh bread into and share with some friends.

Food Landscapes

Stroll through the land of other people's food
Hear stories of the offerings they have made
to those they love
Imagine tastes and breathe in the aromas of
their memories
As though they have already been told and heard
so many times
or never told at all but on the edge of all tongues
waiting forever to be told

Because it is a necessity
to share the deepest excited expression of love
the most basic complexity
the building blocks of human existential anatomy

and unaware the cook recounts with simple glee
and temperament

It happened everywhere and always, that is the
exception I noted
Inducing me to ask more,
and go to that place of all beginnings with others
because it makes both them and me happy to
speak and to listen
But more than anything to be in touch for that one
moment with that real thing that they have shared
one time in love

Paying Tribute to the Fried Stuff

Deep frying at home is one of the most arduous of cooking processes, and also one of the most challenging if you are not using an electric fryer. Life speeds up when you are frying, so you must be attentive and watchful. A lot happens simultaneously: the dredging, the oil spurting, the ingredient reaching its cooking point. Often, as one piece is added to the oil, another needs to be removed. The process is messy, but rewarding.

Fried Vegetables

serves · 4 to 6   time · Under 1 hour

Salt and pepper

1 pound (500 grams) zucchini and/or eggplants, very thinly sliced

2½ cups (300 grams) all-purpose flour

1½ cups (350 milliliters) ouzo or any other clear liquor (gin, vodka, etc.)

Sunflower oil

tip

You will not taste ouzo in the final dish—the ouzo is actually what gives the vegetables their delicate crunchy crust.

Salt the zucchini and/or eggplants well and let sit in a colander for 20 to 30 minutes to extract excess moisture.

Place the flour on a plate or in a shallow dish and pour the ouzo into a shallow bowl. Season the vegetables with pepper, dredge in the flour, and dip into the ouzo.

Fill a deep frying pan with about 1 inch (2.5 centimeters) of oil and place over medium high heat. In order to make sure the oil is hot enough, stick a small piece of vegetable into the oil; if it immediately starts fizzing, then it is hot enough. Place vegetables in the pan and cook, in batches, in the hot oil. Once golden and crisp, transfer the vegetables to a plate lined with paper towels to soak up excess oil.

Serve on small plates as a meze.

Fried Squid

serves • 4 to 6   time • Under 1 hour

2 pounds (1 kilogram) small squid, cleaned and cut in ¼-inch (5-millimeter) rings

3¼ cups (400 grams) all-purpose flour

2 teaspoons baking soda

1½ cups (350 milliliters) extra-virgin olive oil

⅔ cup (150 milliliters) sunflower oil

Salt

3 lemons, cut into wedges

tip

Follow the exact same procedure if you want to fry small fish. The only difference is that you don't need to clean them—they can be eaten whole.

After cleaning and cutting the squid, drain well and place on paper towels to remove excess moisture.

Combine the flour and baking soda and place on a plate or shallow dish. Combine the oils in a large, deep frying pan and place over medium high heat.

Dredge the squid in the flour mixture, shaking off excess, and place in the hot oil. In order to make sure the oil is hot enough, stick a small edge of the squid into the oil; if it immediately starts fizzing, then it is hot enough. Fill the frying pan half-full with squid. Cover with a lid. Once the squid is golden brown, transfer to a plate lined with paper towels and salt generously while still hot. Repeat this process until you have fried all of the squid. Add more oil to the frying pan as needed, letting it heat up before adding more squid.

Serve on a plate with big wedges of lemon.

Traganisti Araviki Pita

PITA BREAD CRISPS

These chip-like crackers are something we always have in the cupboard, stored in one of the tins my mother so passionately collects (usually the dark green one from an Italian panettone). I am so used to having them around that I almost forgot to include the recipe in this collection! We serve them with all types of meze and dips, or eat them like homemade chips.

serves • 8 to 10   time • Under 1 hour

6 large pita breads

1¼ cups (300 milliliters) extra-virgin olive oil

4 tablespoons dried rosemary, crumbled

Salt

Preheat the oven to 350°F (180°C).

Start by separating each pita bread into two rounds. Pour the olive oil into a bowl and add the rosemary. Using a pastry brush, generously brush the pieces of pita bread with oil on both sides. The trick is to spread the oil out evenly, without leaving the sides of the pita bread dry and without making pools in the center.

Line baking sheets with parchment paper and place a single layer of pita bread on each sheet.

Bake until golden brown, 7 to 10 minutes. Keep an eye on them, as they can easily overcook. The moment they come out of the oven, season well with salt.

Once cool, break into smaller pieces and store in an airtight container. They will last for 2 weeks or more. Dip them into almost anything, or eat them as is for a quick snack.

Melitzanes Laderes

OVEN-BAKED EGGPLANT

If you have a vegetable garden, the summer months are a time to exult in the bounty you have at hand. Too much produce can be an incentive to try new recipes and create new ways to consume everything. That is, unless you love a dish so much (as I love this one) that you just want to make the same recipe over and over again.   serves • 4 to 6   time • Under 4 hours

4 large eggplants

Salt and pepper

Extra-virgin olive oil

1 large onion, finely chopped

2 cloves garlic, crushed

2 green bell peppers,
   finely chopped

1 red bell pepper, finely chopped

10 tomatoes, grated, or one
   28-ounce (800-gram) can
   diced tomatoes

1/2 cup chopped parsley leaves
   (about 1/2 bunch)

Sugar

4 tablespoons breadcrumbs

4 ounces (110 grams)
   feta cheese

Cut the eggplants into slices about 3/4 inch (1.5 centimeters) thick and place a colander in the sink or put a plate underneath to catch the liquid released by the eggplants. Sprinkle very generously with salt and let sit for 1½ to 2 hours. (This is done to remove bitterness from the eggplants.)

Meanwhile, make the tomato sauce: Cover the bottom of a medium deep frying pan with olive oil, and add the onion and garlic with a pinch of salt. Cook over medium heat until the onion is soft and translucent, then add the bell peppers. Patiently allow time for the vegetables to caramelize and for their flavors to blend.

Add the tomatoes and 3/4 cup (180 milliliters) of water. Bring to a rolling boil, then lower the heat and simmer until the sauce has thickened substantially, about 20 minutes. Add the parsley and season with sugar, salt, and pepper. Taste, and adjust the acidity by adding a pinch or more of sugar until the sauce is balanced.

Preheat the oven to 350°F (180°C).

Rinse the eggplants and pat dry with paper towels. Line two baking sheets with parchment paper. Place a single layer of eggplant slices on the sheets. Brush both sides with olive oil and season with pepper and a small pinch of sugar.

Bake in the oven for about 1 hour, until the eggplants are soft and juicy. If you notice any slices drying out, brush with a little more oil and sprinkle the tray with water. Remove from the oven and let cool.

Spread a spoonful of sauce over the bottom of a baking dish, then add a layer of eggplants, placing slices close to one another and filling gaps with smaller pieces. Continue to layer sauce, then eggplants, until all ingredients have been used, finishing with sauce. Sprinkle the breadcrumbs over the top.

Bake in the oven for 30 minutes. Just before serving, crumble feta cheese on top and serve in the baking dish.

Psito Psari

GRILLED OR BROILED FISH

Kyria Loula was a person with immediate access to raw emotions, having never been taught to be ashamed of them. I liked the way she talked about my family's past with untamed emotion. There was a simplicity to her expressions that I admired, just like I admire the simplicity in Greek food.

serves • 4 to 6   time • Under 3 hours

One (5- to 6-pound / 2- to 3-kilogram) whole fish, such as grouper, sea bream, or sea bass

Extra-virgin olive oil

Salt and pepper

Dried oregano

Juice of 1 to 2 lemons

ladolemono (optional)

Juice of 1 to 2 lemons

1 cup (250 milliliters) extra-virgin olive oil

Salt and pepper

1 recipe Mayonnaise (page 214; optional)

tip

The cooking time depends greatly on your oven and the size of your fish, so check frequently. Overcooked fish is a distressing affair!

Clean the fish or ask your fishmonger to do it for you.

Place the fish in a baking dish and generously drizzle with oil. Rub all over with plenty of salt, pepper, and oregano, and then splash with lemon juice. Marinate for 2 hours.

Prepare your grill for high heat or preheat your broiler (removing the broiler rack before preheating).

Once the grill or broiler is to temperature, brush the grill grate or broiler rack well with oil. If grilling, cook for 15 minutes on either side (do not flip it more than once). If broiling, place the fish on the rack with a baking sheet underneath to catch the drippings from the fish, and cook for about 30 minutes.

Test to see if the fish is ready by pressing the meat with your finger—it should be soft but firm and give a little when pressed. If the fish shows some resistance, your finger almost bouncing off its flesh, it is still raw; if the flesh feels hard, take it out of the oven immediately—it is in danger of being overcooked.

If using, while the fish is cooking, make the ladolemono (oil and lemon sauce) that we use to accompany broiled or grilled fish. Pour the lemon juice and 1 cup of olive oil into a jar, cover with the lid, and shake until it comes together into a light yellow, thick liquid. Season with some salt and pepper and set aside (if it separates, just give it another shake and it will come together again). You may also make the mayonnaise as instructed on page 214.

Serve the fish whole, on a platter with the sauces.

Charlotte's Potato Salad

I have generally avoided adding the names of those who contributed their recipes to the recipe titles in this book, but some, like this one, just have to be named. I can't think of this salad without thinking of Charlotte, my mother. What I remember most is her perfectionism in achieving precisely the flavor she wants. Charlotte's character is an invaluable ingredient of this potato salad.

serves • 4 to 6   time • Under 2 hours

8 medium to large potatoes

Salt and pepper

4 hard-boiled eggs, peeled and quartered

9 ounces (250 grams) feta cheese

1 small onion, sliced in half moons

1 recipe Mayonnaise (page 214)

½ cup coarsely chopped parsley leaves (about ½ bunch)

Boil the whole, unpeeled potatoes in heavily salted water until fork-tender. Drain well. Once just cool enough to handle, peel and cut potatoes into about six pieces each, making sure they are all about the same size.

Place the potatoes and quartered eggs into a large bowl. Crumble the feta over the bowl and add the onion, mayonnaise, parsley, salt, and pepper. Toss together and taste, adjusting the seasoning, if necessary. Place in the fridge to cool for 1 hour before serving.

Kolokithopita

ZUCCHINI PIE

If you master a kolokithopita, you have mastered the world of pies; substitute any other vegetable for the zucchini and replace the mint and dill with other herbs. Make this for a light lunch, take it on a picnic, or give it to your children as a packed lunch for school. Pieces of cold pie were one of my favorite things to eat at school—never did junk food grace my lunch box!

serves • 6 to 8   time • Under 2 hours

6 to 7 medium zucchini (about 2 pounds / 1 kilogram), grated

Salt and pepper

Extra-virgin olive oil

1 onion, grated

5 ounces (150 grams) crumbled feta cheese

1/2 cup (125 grams) anthotyro or ricotta cheese

3 large eggs

1/2 cup finely chopped dill (about 1/2 bunch)

2 tablespoons dried mint

One 8-ounce (225-gram) package phyllo dough

tip

You can make this pie ahead. Freeze just before baking, and bake for 1½ hours from the freezer. If the phyllo goes golden brown before the pie has fully baked, cover it with a loose layer of foil, then uncover it for the last 5 minutes.

Place the grated zucchini in a colander in the sink or over a plate. Salt well to bring out excess moisture, and let it sit while you prepare the other ingredients.

Coat a small frying pan with a thin layer of oil and place over medium heat. Add the onion and cook until just starting to brown. Remove from the heat, place in a large bowl, and let cool.

Preheat the oven to 350°F (180°C).

Crumble the cheeses over the onion, add the eggs and herbs, and season with salt and pepper. Add the zucchini. Adjust seasoning to taste.

Brush a 13-by-9-inch (33-by-23-centimeter) baking dish or pan with olive oil. Start the pie by laying a phyllo sheet on all four sides of the baking dish. Each sheet should partially cover the bottom of the dish, with the rest hanging over the edge. Brush every piece of phyllo that you lay on the dish with oil. Then place five sheets in the center, brushing each with oil. Add the filling and spread it out evenly.

Place five more sheets of phyllo over the filling, then fold over the overhanging sheets that you started with. Cut any excess phyllo away with scissors or a knife and use your pastry brush to tuck the phyllo in around the edges of the dish. Score the top with a sharp knife, marking the pieces you wish to cut later. Sprinkle with a little water.

Bake in the oven for 45 minutes to 1 hour, or until the phyllo is a deep golden brown.

Vrasta Lahanika

BOILED VEGETABLES

Boiled vegetables were almost like milk in our house. They were always around, unless the last of the batch had just been finished. They were always seasonal, and one season's vegetables were gladly followed by the harvest of the next. They keep up to about five days in the fridge.   serves • 2 to 3   time • Under 30 minutes

1½ pounds (650 grams) vegetables, such as zucchini, green beans, beets, cauliflower, broccoli, or greens (such as dandelion or chard)

Extra-virgin olive oil

Lemon juice or vinegar

Salt and pepper

Bring a pot of heavily salted water to a boil, add the vegetables, and cook until a fork can pierce them easily and the center is still firm. Strain, then submerge in a bowl with iced water to lower the temperature immediately. Transfer to a bowl and refrigerate. Serve cold, accompanied with olive oil, lemon juice or vinegar, and pepper. Let each person season his or her own vegetables.

Svigous

FRIED DOUGH BALLS WITH SYRUP

"They puff open just like flowers, and turn as though an invisible hand is there to gently roll them to the other side. I loved standing over the frying pan to watch them open." With this remembrance, Kyria Loula was transported from her bedridden state to our family's kitchen. I, in turn, imagined her slight body hunched over the frying pan—as I had seen her many times before—completely absorbed in the process.   makes • 36 to 40 balls   time • Under 1 hour

1 cup (2 sticks) plus
  2 tablespoons (250 grams)
  unsalted butter

Pinch salt

1 cup plus 2 tablespoons
  (140 grams) all-purpose flour

1 teaspoon baking powder

6 large eggs

syrup

3 tablespoons sugar

2 tablespoons honey

1 cinnamon stick

3 cloves

1 strip of lemon zest

Sunflower or corn oil, for frying

5 tablespoons ground cinnamon

Combine 1 cup plus 2 tablespoons (275 milliliters) water, the butter, and salt in a saucepan over medium heat. Once the butter has melted and the water is boiling, add the flour and baking powder and stir, using a wooden spoon. Stir constantly until the mixture is smooth and pulls away from the sides of the pan. Remove from the heat and transfer to a bowl to cool.

Once the mixture is cool, add the eggs, one by one, beating with a whisk after each addition. The dough should be shiny and smooth.

Make the syrup: Combine all the ingredients for the syrup with ¾ cup (180 milliliters) water in a small saucepan over low heat. Let it reach a gentle boil, then boil for 15 minutes.

Meanwhile, add 2 inches (5 centimeters) sunflower oil to a medium saucepan over medium high heat. To make sure the oil is hot enough, drop a small ball of dough into the oil; it should immediately start fizzing. Once hot, add 4 separate teaspoons of dough and cook until they turn a golden color on all sides. Stir with a slotted spoon to ensure that the dough balls color on all sides. Transfer them to a plate with paper towels to drain. Repeat with remaining dough, cooking in batches of four.

Cover the bottom of a round platter with a thin layer of cinnamon. Arrange the dough balls, in layers, to form a mountain shape on the platter; before starting each new layer, top with some syrup and sprinkle with cinnamon.

Baklava

This recipe travels to you from the village where my great-grandfather went to school, deep in the Greek mainland. Every time my great-uncle and -aunt visited, they were invited into the home of a local family and served this baklava.

Baklava is made with different nuts, depending on whatever a particular region produces—this variation is made with walnuts.

serves • 8 to 10   time • Under 2 hours

4 cups (about 1 pound / 500 grams) finely chopped walnuts

2½ cups plus 1½ tablespoons (525 grams) granulated sugar

1½ teaspoons ground cinnamon

1 teaspoon ground cloves

6 tablespoons extra-virgin olive oil, plus more for brushing

One 8-ounce (225-gram) package phyllo dough

Whole cloves, to decorate (optional)

Combine the walnuts, 1½ tablespoons sugar, cinnamon, and cloves. Brush the bottom and sides of a 13-by-9-inch (33-by-23-centimeter) glass baking dish or metal cake pan with a thin layer of olive oil and cut the phyllo pastry to the size of the dish. Add one sheet of phyllo, brush with olive oil, and repeat with another two sheets. Continue layering with phyllo sheets, brushing each with olive oil, and scattering each one with the walnut mixture. Repeat this until no walnut mixture remains, then top with a final phyllo sheet. Be sure not to pack the phyllo down tightly so that the baklava ends up being light and crispy.

Preheat the oven to 325°F (170°C).

Cut the baklava into diamond-shaped pieces. Stick a whole clove into the center of each piece, if desired. Heat 6 tablespoons of olive oil in a small saucepan until nearly smoking and pour over the baklava.

Bake in the oven for about 1 hour, or until the phyllo is a beautiful golden brown.

Meanwhile, combine the remaining 2½ cups sugar and 1 cup (250 milliliters) water in a saucepan and bring to a boil. Simmer for 8 to 10 minutes, then allow to cool. If you stick the back of a spoon into it, then draw a line with your finger on the back of the spoon and the syrup doesn't drip, it is ready.

Pour the cooled syrup over the baklava while still piping hot. Cool completely before serving and cutting.

Chocolate Mousse

Few things excite people as much as chocolate, but as a non-crazed chocolate eater, I look upon blind faith in chocolate with disapproval; avid fans who often lose their ability to think critically in the face of chocolate are something of a mystery to me. This is not to say that I don't find chocolate a wonderful ingredient!

You will notice that this mousse comprises two ingredients: eggs and chocolate. To those accustomed to whipped-cream chocolate mousse, this dish may seem eggy, but in my opinion, the light texture given by the beaten egg whites cannot be surpassed.   serves • 4   time • Under 3 hours

3½ ounces (100 grams) bittersweet chocolate, chopped

4 large eggs, separated

1 tablespoon liquor or liqueur of choice (brandy, Grand Marnier, Baileys; optional)

Pinch salt

2 tablespoons grated dark chocolate, to decorate (optional)

tip

Add 2 to 3 tablespoons of granulated sugar if you want a sweeter dessert.

tip

You can use this mousse to fill a simple sponge cake or the Christmas Chocolate Log (page 199), or as an alternative to the buttercream in the Layered Chocolate Birthday Cake (page 177).

Melt the bittersweet chocolate in a double boiler or small saucepan, stirring constantly until it melts. Remove from the heat and let cool slightly.

Beat the egg yolks until pale and thick enough to drop off a spoon in a ribbon-like fashion. Use a spatula to gently fold together the cooled melted chocolate and the yolks until well combined. Add the liquor or liqueur, if using.

Beat the egg whites, with a pinch of salt, to stiff peaks. If you can turn your bowl upside down and the egg whites stay in the bowl, they're ready.

Fold the egg whites gently into the chocolate mixture, taking care not to lose too much air. Make sure you do not leave any pockets of egg white unmixed in your attempt to maintain fluffiness! Transfer the mousse to one large serving bowl, or into individual dessert glasses.

Chill in the fridge for at least 2 hours, until the mousse comes together to become the glorious dessert it was meant to be. Just before serving, sprinkle with the grated chocolate, if you wish.

Traditions

This chapter is dedicated to the annual traditions we observed in my family as I was growing up. Most of these occasions are rooted in history, religion, or nature; but what makes them significant to me are the memories of my family coming together, and the core respect for process that characterized the preparations.

My parents are responsible for upholding each and every one of the traditions in this section; and the beauty of it is that I don't think this was ever a calculated decision. I don't think they consciously decided to create a tradition out of making a birthday cake, kneading tsoureki, making jam at the end of the strawberry season, or preparing the lamb for Easter. I believe they both just shared the same respect for routine and ceremony. Whatever the reason, I am ever grateful for these consistent moments of reunion that I looked forward to throughout the year.

Though Easter is the time I associate most with extended family gatherings, I have not been able to give it the presence it deserves in this chapter, as a lot of the dishes are difficult to make outside of Greece. I have organized this chapter in chronological order to illustrate how each year of my childhood was split into days of "celebration," starting with New Year's Day and ending with New Year's Eve.

Feel free to pick your own days of the year to cook and to eat any of these recipes—and if you love them so much that you don't have the patience to wait until next year, you can make them any time you want (though this may diminish their magic!). Perhaps you will choose to create traditions of your own by picking your favorite recipes and making them on days that are significant to your family. The anticipation that grows throughout the year makes the day you taste the meal again—as well as all the preparations that surround it—all the more memorable.

Vasilopita

NEW YEAR'S CAKE

Make the cake. Sprinkle it with powdered sugar. Stick a coin wrapped in foil in the bottom of the cake and give it a few spins until you become disoriented and can't figure out where you put the coin. Decide how many pieces you will cut—it must be an even number. Pick different things to which you want to bring luck: your dog, your work, your house, your country, your whatever. Waste more time than necessary arguing about the pieces and then begin dividing the cake by cutting lightly on the surface. Start by making a cross, blessing the cake—a tradition left over from more religious times—and then divide each quarter by cutting across the whole cake. Be sure to cut the pieces evenly to make sure all pieces have an equal chance of winning the coin, as whoever wins will have luck for the year to come. In my family, the coin is always a lucky charm that can be worn as a bracelet or necklace or used as a key chain, so that the lucky person can carry their good luck around everywhere they go!

serves • As many as needed   time • Under 2 hours

¾ cup (1½ sticks / 170 grams) unsalted butter, room temperature

¾ cup (150 grams) granulated sugar

3 large eggs

Zest of 1 orange

6 tablespoons (90 milliliters) orange juice

2¼ cups (280 grams) all-purpose flour

2 teaspoons baking powder

½ teaspoon baking soda

½ teaspoon salt

6 tablespoons (90 milliliters) milk

⅓ cup (80 milliliters) brandy

Powdered sugar, for dusting

Preheat the oven to 350°F (180°C). Grease and flour a 10-inch (25-centimeter) round springform cake pan.

Using an electric mixer, beat the butter and the granulated sugar together until light and fluffy. Add the eggs, one at a time, beating after each addition. Beat in the orange zest and juice.

Sift together the flour, baking powder, baking soda, and salt. Combine the milk and brandy. Alternately add the flour mixture and the milk mixture to the butter mixture, beating after each addition. Pour the batter into the prepared cake pan.

Bake in the oven for about 45 minutes to 1 hour, until a knife inserted in the center comes out clean. Once cool, remove the outer ring from the pan, place a cutting board on top of the cake, and flip over. Carefully remove the bottom of the cake pan. Dust with powdered sugar and serve.

Layered Chocolate Birthday Cake

My mother was a working mother with little free time at her disposal. But whether it was sharing breakfast every day, Sunday lunch every week, or birthday cakes every year, she made sure to create and uphold consistent and memorable rituals with us. Three days before my birthday, I knew where to find her: in the kitchen, working away on my cake. The kitchen was off limits for those prep days, and as my birthday neared, the enchantment increased for everyone in the house. By the time the candles were lit, my excitement was converted into prideful birthday smugness. I looked forward to seeing what form she had decided to give my cake; once it was a piano, another time it was a chest filled with gummy treasure, and another, a paint palette. Her cakes were the best.

serves • 8 to 10   time • Under 2 hours (plus time for decorating)

3 ounces (85 grams) bittersweet chocolate, chopped

½ cup (1 stick / 120 grams) unsalted butter, room temperature

1 cup plus 2 tablespoons (225 grams) granulated sugar

2 large eggs

2½ tablespoons white wine vinegar

1⅓ cups (165 grams) all-purpose flour, sifted

1 teaspoon baking powder

1 teaspoon baking soda

½ teaspoon salt

¾ cup (180 milliliters) milk

1 recipe Chocolate Buttercream (recipe follows)

1 recipe Decorating Icing (recipe follows)

Preheat the oven to 375°F (190°C). Grease a 10-inch (25-centimeter) round springform cake pan with butter and dust with flour. Bang it upside down on your work surface to remove excess flour.

Melt the chocolate in a double boiler or small saucepan, stirring constantly until it melts. Remove from the heat and let cool.

Cream the butter with the sugar using an electric mixer, then beat in the eggs one at a time. Mix in the vinegar and the cooled melted chocolate. Combine the flour, baking powder, baking soda, and salt and start adding to the chocolate mixture, alternating with the milk. Tip the cake mixture into the prepared cake pan.

Bake in the oven for 35 to 40 minutes. Make sure it doesn't get too dry; the magic of this cake is its fudgy, soft texture. Remove from the oven and let cool.

Once cool, remove the outer ring from the pan, place a cutting board on top of the cake, and flip over. Carefully remove the bottom of the cake pan. Cut the cake into two layers with a serrated knife. Spread the chocolate buttercream between the layers. Use icing to decorate the top of the cake as you wish.

Chocolate Buttercream

This recipe fills the chocolate birthday cake generously.

<u>makes</u> • 4 cups (950 milliliters)

8 ounces (225 grams) bittersweet chocolate, chopped

1 tablespoon instant coffee

2 tablespoons boiling water

4 large egg yolks

1½ cups (190 grams) powdered sugar

Pinch salt

1½ cups (3 sticks / 340 grams) unsalted butter, room temperature

Melt the chocolate as you did for the cake, and set aside to cool. Dissolve the coffee in the boiling water.

Beat the yolks with the sugar until thick, using an electric mixer. While beating, add the dissolved coffee in two parts and then the melted chocolate and salt. Keep beating on low speed and add the butter, 2 tablespoons at a time. The buttercream should now have a light brown color and an airy texture.

Decorating Icing

<u>makes</u> • 5 cups (1.2 liters)

2 large egg whites, room temperature

1 cup (125 grams) powdered sugar

¼ teaspoon cream of tartar

Combine the egg whites, sugar, 5 tablespoons water, and cream of tartar in a glass or stainless-steel bowl. Place a large pot of water over medium heat. Once it starts steaming (do not let it boil), place the bowl in the water and beat constantly with an electric mixer for 7 minutes until the icing is thick, smooth, and shiny.

tip

Add natural food coloring to make the icing any color you wish, to match the theme of your cake.

Bakaliaros Tiganitos

DEEP-FRIED SALT COD

Salt cod, as you can imagine, is incredibly salty. The most important part of this recipe is to soak the fish thoroughly in water to remove the excess salt. If you cut corners, you will end up with beautiful golden fried cod pieces that are impossible to eat!

In my family, we eat this dish once a year, on March 25. Though this is during Lent, the Greek Orthodox Church allows its followers to eat fish (normally not consumed during this time) to celebrate the Feast of the Annunciation; coming from a family that was not actively religious, this was not something I knew while growing up! As for why we don't make it at other times during the year, we save it to rejoice in the reunion all the more.

serves • 6 to 7   time • Under 2 hours (plus soaking)

1 salt cod fillet (about
1½ pounds / 700 grams)

2 cups (250 grams) all-purpose
flour, plus more for dredging

One 12-ounce (330-milliliter)
can beer

White pepper

Sunflower or corn oil

1 recipe Mayonnaise (page 214;
optional)

1 recipe Skordalia (page 183;
optional)

Place the salt cod in a bowl, cover with cold water, and let soak in the refrigerator for 18 to 24 hours, changing the water as often as you can.

One hour before frying, put the flour in a large bowl and slowly add the beer, mixing well. The mixture should be thick enough to cover the cod, but thin enough for the excess batter to slide off easily. If you have added all the beer and the batter is still too thick, add a little water and mix well. Season to taste with white pepper. Cover and let sit in the fridge until needed. Strain the cod and cut into pieces, about 1½ inches (3.5 centimeters) long, removing any bones. Pat dry with paper towels and set aside.

Add ½ inch (1 centimeter) oil to a large, deep frying pan and heat until very hot and nearly smoking (about 380°F/190°C).

Test the oil temperature by dredging a small piece of fish in flour, dipping it into the batter with the help of a wooden skewer or toothpick, shaking to remove excess batter, and adding it to the oil. It should bubble immediately. If it doesn't bubble, increase the temperature. If it takes on color too quickly, turn down the burner and allow the oil to cool a bit before retesting.

Line a plate with plenty of paper towels. Dredge each piece of fish according to the above directions and add to the hot oil and fry for 3½ to 4 minutes, or until the batter turns a nice dark golden brown. (For ease, you can leave the toothpick in the cod while it fries and take it out once out of the oil.) Prepare and add a few more pieces of cod to the pan. Do not crowd your frying pan; it will lower the temperature of the oil substantially. Once cooked, transfer to the paper towel–lined plate to drain. Fry the remaining cod, in batches, replacing the oil if it gets dark or full of too many burned bits.

Serve on a platter piled high accompanied by mayonnaise and/or skordalia.

Skordalia

GARLIC DIP

An indication of knowing someone really well is knowing which foods they love, like, and hate. My father loves this recipe, and I was told by Kyria Loula, who knew him as a boy, that it had to go into the book just for him. If you follow his taste buds, the more garlic the better. If you follow mine, start slow, taste as you go, and add more garlic as needed.   <u>makes</u> • 2 cups   <u>time</u> • Under 30 minutes

½ small potato, peeled

Salt and pepper

2 cloves garlic, or to taste

1 teaspoon sea salt

2 slices bread, crusts removed and slices soaked in water

½ cup (60 grams) almonds, toasted

Juice of 1 lemon

1 cup (250 milliliters) extra-virgin olive oil

Kyria Loula advised that if the skordalia separates, add an ice cube and keep blending.

Boil the potato in a small pot of salted water.

Add the 2 cloves of garlic and sea salt to a blender or food processor, and pulse until it becomes a thick paste. Add more garlic if desired. Squeeze the water from the bread, and drain the potato, reserving some of the cooking water. Add the bread and potato to the garlic paste along with the almonds and half the lemon juice. Process until the mixture is well combined, but still slightly coarse in texture.

While the processor is running, start to slowly pour the olive oil into the mixture. If it is too thick, add a spoonful of the reserved potato water and continue to add the oil. Once the mixture becomes lighter in color and thinner in texture, stop and taste your creation. Season with salt and pepper to taste, and add a little of the remaining lemon juice. Taste again, and if you are lucky enough to have gotten it just right, put into a bowl or jar and reserve in the fridge for up to 1 week.

If the skordalia seems unbalanced, use your taste buds to steer you in the right direction. If you want it more pungent, add more garlic. If the garlic flavor is overpowering, add a few drops of lemon juice. Season with more salt. Blend. Taste again. Repeat as many times as needed to get it where you want it. Skordalia needs to taste good to you, not to me.

Koulourakia

EASTER BUTTER COOKIES

In her attempt to make sure these cookies last until Easter day, my mother hides them away from view. They are so soft and finely textured that we (specifically my brother) eat them by the handful, and she worries that there will be none left for our Easter guests. We laugh at her protective spirit because she ends up being mean in the name of goodness. We eat these cookies with a dollop of whipped cream and a fresh strawberry on top, or with a small chocolate Easter egg.

makes • 65 cookies   time • Under 2 hours

1 cup (2 sticks / 230 grams) unsalted butter, cubed, room temperature

¾ cup (100 grams) powdered sugar

1 large egg

1 teaspoon vanilla extract

1 teaspoon baking powder

4 cups (500 grams) all-purpose flour

If you want a shiny finish, brush on beaten egg or milk before baking.

Add to the experience by dipping half the cookie into melted dark chocolate. Allow the chocolate to harden before serving.

In a large bowl, cream together the butter and powdered sugar until pale and fluffy, using either an electric mixer or a wooden spoon. Add the egg and continue mixing.

Add the vanilla and baking powder. Finally, add the flour, little by little, mixing after each addition, until a soft and smooth dough is formed (if it comes together into a smooth dough and stops sticking to the sides of the bowl before you finish adding all the flour, stop adding the flour!). Once the dough is ready, wrap it in parchment paper and set it aside in the fridge for at least 30 minutes.

Preheat the oven to 375°F (190°C). Line two baking sheets with parchment paper.

Use your hands to form the koulourakia by rolling the dough into 2- to 3-inch (5- to 7.5-centimeter) snakes (the size depends on how important it is to you to make them delicately small). Overlap the two ends to form a loose circle. They need to be bite-size when raw so that they can expand to the perfect size while baking. Place on the prepared baking sheets.

Bake in the oven until they are a beautiful golden color, 15 to 20 minutes.

Tsoureki

EASTER BREAD

I love kneading dough and find it highly therapeutic. Making this bread was another yearly tradition my mother upheld in our home: every Thursday before Easter Sunday, the sour smell of yeast inundated the house, large quantities of dough were kneaded in plastic basins, and time changed to accommodate the process of the recipe. Then, on Easter Sunday morning we gathered to eat a breakfast of tsoureki with jam or anthotyro (a ricotta-like cheese) and honey; the men rose early to prepare the lamb on a spit for lunch, so it was usually just us children with the women of the family sitting at the table.

serves • 3 to 4   time • Under 4 hours

¾ ounce (20 grams) fresh yeast

⅓ cup (65 grams) plus
1½ teaspoons granulated
sugar

⅓ cup (75 milliliters) milk

2 cups (250 grams) bread flour

½ teaspoon salt

½ teaspoon ground mahlab

¼ teaspoon ground mastic

Zest of 1 orange

1 large egg plus 1 large egg yolk,
beaten

4 tablespoons (55 grams)
unsalted butter, melted

Mix the yeast with 1½ teaspoons of sugar until it becomes liquid. Heat the milk until it feels warm but not hot against your skin (about 105°F/40°C). Add two-thirds of it to the yeast mixture, along with ⅓ cup (30 grams) of flour. Mix well and cover with a tea towel. Let it rise in a warm place until the mixture doubles in size and bubbles appear on the surface.

Mix the remaining 1⅔ cups (220 grams) flour, ⅓ cup (65 grams) sugar, salt, mahlab, mastic, and orange zest together with a whisk. Add the whole egg, the remaining milk, and half the melted butter. Knead with your hands, or mix on low with a stand mixer fitted with a dough hook, until the dough starts coming together.

Once the yeast mixture has doubled in volume, add it to the dough along with the other half of the butter. Knead for at least 15 minutes by hand, or 10 minutes in the mixer, until the dough is soft, smooth, and does not stick to the sides of the bowl.

Cover the bowl with a cloth or seal with plastic wrap and let rise in a warm place without drafts for approximately 2 hours.

When doubled in size, knead the dough once or twice by hand, shape into an oval ball, or separate into three pieces, roll them out into strands, and braid them together. Place on a baking sheet lined with parchment paper and let rise, uncovered, for another 45 minutes.

Preheat the oven to 350°F (180°C).

Brush the dough with the beaten egg yolk and bake for 35 to 40 minutes in the oven on the middle rack, until it is golden brown and a knife comes out clean. Cover with foil if the top starts turning dark brown before the bread is baked.

Serve in slices (toasted or not) with jam, butter or anthotyro (or ricotta), and honey.

Revithada

OVEN-BAKED CHICKPEA SOUP

I include this recipe for my uncle Nico, whose most unique attribute, in my eyes, is his unabashed way of showing and sharing his pride of country, family, birthplace, friends, and more . . . Unlike many of my other family members who hold back such emotions, he just shouts his pride to the world, and this I admire.

Uncle Nico is from the Cycladic island of Sifnos, as is this dish; even if I have no particular ties to this recipe—apart from the fact that I absolutely love the taste—to omit it from this book would be to omit the part of my family experience that he represents.

This dish is baked in a beautiful ceramic dish with a lid, called a *tsoukali*, that can be found in many shapes, sizes, and colors. I was told by Nico's daughter Amalia that in Sifnos, revithada was eaten every Sunday for breakfast. Each household prepared its own batch that was taken to the local bakery to be baked in the wood oven for hours until Sunday morning when the woman of the house went to retrieve it and bring it home to the family for a feast. There is something nostalgic about eating a dish that traditionally involved a whole community and was enjoyed, without fail, every week. Please cook this to honor your origins, family, and everything in which you take pride.

serves • 5 to 6   time • Under 4 hours (plus soaking overnight)

One 1-pound (500-gram) package dried chickpeas

2 tablespoons baking soda

1 large onion, chopped

¾ cup finely chopped dill (about 1 bunch)

Salt and pepper

Extra-virgin olive oil

tip

The traditional revithada recipe doesn't call for dill, so feel free to omit it—but I find it works amazingly well with the chickpeas!

Soak the chickpeas in water for at least 12 hours, changing the water every so often.

Drain well, sprinkle with baking soda, rub the chickpeas around with your hands to ensure they are completely covered in baking soda, and set aside for 20 minutes. Fill the bowl with water, then watch as the skins rise to the surface. Drain the chickpeas, discarding the skins. Rinse well under running water, rubbing the chickpeas to remove any stubborn skins.

Preheat the oven to 320°F (160°C).

Put the chickpeas in a large pot over high heat and cover with water. Bring to a boil. Skim off the white foam that rises to the surface and remove from the heat when there's no more foam rising to the top.

Drain the chickpeas and place in a ceramic baking dish with a lid. Add the onion, half of the dill, some salt and pepper, a generous amount of olive oil, and enough water to barely cover the chickpeas.

Bake in the oven, covered, for 3 hours. Check every so often to see if it needs any extra water. The chickpeas should be soft, but still intact. Once ready, sprinkle with the remaining dill and serve.

tip

If you can't find a ceramic casserole dish to bake this in, just use a heavy, oven-safe metal pot with a lid. If you must use a standard baking dish without a lid, cover with foil. However, it will take less time and more moisture will evaporate, so keep a watchful eye on the water and top up as needed.

Strawberry or Apricot Jam

While I was growing up, we always ate homemade jam—either apricot or strawberry—and more often than not, my mother made it herself at the end of the fruit's respective seasons. I remember the process so clearly, all of us huddled in the kitchen, my mother filling the room with her presence. I remember watching for exactly the right moment when everything in the pot—the texture, the color, the taste—converged into the perfect jam. In sharing this recipe with you, I hope to share a little of the joy I felt when making jam in the kitchen with my mother.

makes • 7 half-pint jars   time • Under 2 hours (plus 4 hours or longer for resting)

2 pounds (1 kilogram) very ripe strawberries or apricots

3¾ cups (750 grams) granulated sugar

2 to 3 tablespoons lemon juice

tip

When opening a new jar, check for any signs of mold or bacteria, and discard any jars that look suspicious. Store in the fridge for up to 1 month after opening.

Clean the fruit, hulling the strawberries or removing the pits from the apricots. Take a moment to enjoy the aroma of the ripened fruit.

Combine the fruit and the sugar in a large pot. Let sit overnight or for a minimum of 4 hours.

Ensure the sugar has started to dissolve, and use your hands or a potato masher to mash the fruit. Place over low heat, stirring continuously until the sugar is dissolved. Skim off any foam that rises to the surface.

Increase the heat to medium, bring it to a gentle boil, and then lower the heat to keep it cooking on a steady simmer. Stir continuously throughout the cooking process. Keep a small bowl of water and a slotted spoon next to the pot to collect any foam that rises to the surface.

When you start seeing signs of the fruit's color darkening and becoming caramelized, but still vibrant, remove from the heat.

If the jam wrinkles when touched, it is ready. If not, continue cooking.

Before removing the jam from the heat, stir in the lemon juice and simmer for another 5 minutes. Taste again, making sure you allow it to cool—do not be overeager to taste it, as you can really burn yourself!

Meanwhile, sterilize your jars by submerging them for 2 to 3 minutes, top down, in a pot of boiling water. Carefully remove the jars from the pot and place on a clean tea towel, allowing them to dry completely.

Fill the jars with the hot jam. Use a jam funnel to fill each jar to the very top, then tap on your work surface to release any air. Top off with more jam, if needed, to fill the jar to the very top. Seal with the lid and allow to sit on a tea towel to cool completely (or follow jar manufacturer's guidelines). Label with a name and date, and store in your cupboard.

Oven-Roasted Lamb

The pieces of information I have collected as I made this cookbook are like pieces of a puzzle that had been scattered around my life, waiting to be discovered and put into place. I found that my strong sense of tradition and family, the values I have been brought up with, and my deep sense of respect for process and nature, are all things that have traveled down the genealogical tree from generations gone by.

We eat this roasted lamb on Holy Saturday, the night before Easter Sunday. It is the best alternative to the traditional lamb on a spit, which we devour the next day.   serves · 6 to 8   time · Under 3 hours

Extra-virgin olive oil

1 whole bone-in leg of lamb, about 5½ pounds (2.5 kilograms)

Salt and pepper

¾ cup (180 milliliters) white wine or brandy per 2 pounds (1 kilogram) of lamb

You can lower the oven temperature and roast longer if you have the time. In the words of my great-aunt: "The time that you leave it in the oven can go from 2 hours at 340°F (170°C) to as long as you wish at 300°F (150°C)— you can even forget it there! It will be soft as a loukoumi [Turkish delight]!"

Follow the same procedure to roast a whole or half lamb, or lamb pieces.

Preheat the oven to 340°F (170°C).

Massage a generous amount of olive oil all over the lamb. Combine equal amounts of salt and pepper in a bowl, then rub the seasoning all over the lamb until you think you may have added too much. Place in a shallow roasting pan and cover with foil.

Roast in the oven for 2 hours, checking every 15 minutes after 1½ hours to make sure that you don't surpass the optimal point when the meat is cooked and soft to the touch, but still juicy! Uncover, add the wine or brandy, and return to the oven to roast, uncovered, until the lamb has a golden brown crust. Increase the temperature to 375°F (190°C) for the last 10 minutes.

Serve the lamb on a platter, pouring over any sauce left in the pan after roasting.

Places of Connection

*I travel back to the city of Athens about
seventy years ago.
The city is starting to grow, apartment blocks are
few and scattered. Those living there have not yet
grown that far apart from the life they used to live
outside the city. The memory of being close
to nature's flow is still alive.
It is thus that one, then young man, now older
than he can accept, encounters an old man of 90
ascending the road with a live lamb draped around
his neck. He is returning on foot from the south of
Athens, where there are still hills, goats roaming
freely and shepherds. He has chosen a lamb to
make a meal of. He stands on the minute inside
veranda right behind the kitchen of their apartment
in the center of the city to slaughter and skin with a
sharp penknife and the utmost respect, the animal
he has chosen. No one is deemed skillful enough to
replace him unless life decides it is time. He believes
others barbaric, devoid of precision and skill,
full of potential to injure and mistreat the lamb
he will then eat.*

*They say, that this old man is my great-great-
grandfather. This story moves me. It gives me a
sense of true belonging, not to a physical place or
family but to a place within me that is the same as
the place within him that drives him to this ritual
act; and it is this place that I call home.*

Christmas Stuffing

The paradoxical nature of this stuffing is that you do not use it to stuff anything. It is served in a bowl-like platter and accompanied by everything else you serve at your Christmas table. My favorite part of eating it is falling upon a soft, juicy prune that has taken on some of the flavors of the meat.

serves • 8 to 10   time • Under 2 hours

1 tablespoon unsalted butter, plus more for finishing dish

2 onions, finely chopped

Salt and pepper

1 pound (500 grams) ground beef

1 turkey liver, chopped

¾ cup (180 milliliters) brandy

¾ cup (180 milliliters) red wine

1 large tomato, grated

1 tart apple, peeled and grated

Chicken Stock (page 211) or water, as needed

¾ cup (100 grams) raisins

6 prunes, pitted and halved

1½ cups (200 grams) boiled or roasted and shelled chestnuts

⅔ cup (80 grams) pine nuts, toasted

Melt the tablespoon of butter in a deep frying pan over medium heat. Add the onions and a pinch of salt, and cook until soft and translucent. Increase the heat and add the beef and liver, breaking up the beef with a spoon. Cook until browned.

Add the brandy and boil until all the alcohol evaporates, then add the wine, and do the same. Add the tomato, apple, salt, and pepper, and add stock or water to cover. Bring to a boil, then lower the heat and simmer for 45 minutes.

Add the raisins, prunes, chestnuts, and pine nuts, and season to taste. Simmer for a further 45 minutes, adding stock or water if the mixture becomes too dry. The stuffing shouldn't be too wet, but should be moist and juicy. Once off the heat, add a big knob of butter and mix well. Taste and season if needed.

Christmas Cookies

These two types of Christmas cookies start high in a pile on a platter and, as the two weeks of Christmas and New Year's go by, the pile gradually diminishes. They end up being the only evidence that Christmas came and went, as we always make more than we can actually eat!

Kourabiethes

makes • 4 dozen cookies   time • Under 3 hours

1 cup (2 sticks) plus 2 tablespoons (250 grams) unsalted butter, room temperature

3¼ cups plus 1 tablespoon (400 grams) powdered sugar

1 large egg yolk

¼ cup raki or vodka

2 cups (250 grams) all-purpose flour

Scant 1 cup (200 grams) finely chopped almonds, toasted

tip

This dough is soft and sticky, so don't add more flour to make it dry. It needs to stick to your hands slightly.

Using an electric mixer, beat the butter until white and fluffy. Add 1 tablespoon powdered sugar, the egg yolk, and alcohol. Beat well.

With the mixer on low speed, start gradually adding the flour. Once the dough is soft, but still slightly sticky, stop adding flour. Add the chopped almonds. Mix for a few seconds more and let rest in the fridge for 20 minutes.

Preheat the oven to 350°F (180°C). Line two baking sheets with parchment paper. Roll the dough into 1-inch (2.5-centimeter) balls—they don't have to be perfectly round. Place ¾ inch (2 centimeters) apart on the prepared baking sheets. Make a small indentation on the top of each ball with your thumb for the powdered sugar.

Bake in the oven for 20 minutes; even if the kourabiethes are not yet golden, don't worry—they will keep cooking for a while after you have taken them out of the oven.

While the kourabiethes are baking, lay out a few sheets of parchment paper on your work surface and dust with some of the powdered sugar. Once you take the kourabiethes out of the oven, immediately place them on the parchment paper and dust the tops generously with remaining powdered sugar. Let cool and arrange on a mound on a plate.

Melomakarona

makes • 80 cookies   time • Under 3 hours

½ cup (125 milliliters) white wine

1 cup (250 milliliters) extra-virgin olive oil

½ cup (1 stick / 125 grams) unsalted butter, room temperature

1⅓ cups (275 grams) granulated sugar

1½ teaspoons ground cinnamon

½ teaspoon ground cloves

Juice and zest of 1 orange

1 tablespoon brandy

4¾ cups (600 grams) all-purpose flour

½ teaspoon baking powder

¾ teaspoon baking soda

1 tablespoon honey

1 cinnamon stick

1 strip of lemon zest

1 cup (100 grams) walnuts, coarsely ground

Boil the wine for a few minutes. Using an electric mixer, beat the oil and butter together on low speed for a few minutes in a medium bowl. Add ⅓ cup (75 grams) sugar, the spices, and the orange juice and zest. Remove the wine from the heat and add to the mixture along with the brandy.

Sift together the flour, baking powder, and baking soda. Gradually add to the wet mixture, stirring with a wooden spoon. The dough should be soft, smooth, and oily. Let it sit in the fridge for 20 minutes.

Preheat the oven to 350°F (180°C). Line two baking sheets with parchment paper.

Take pieces of the dough a little larger than a teaspoon and form into an oval shape. Use your finger to make indentations in the cookie bottoms (this will help the cookies absorb the syrup when you submerge them). Place ¾ inch (2 centimeters) apart on the prepared sheets. Press a fork over the top of each cookie to make indentations.

Bake in the oven for 40 minutes, until a dark golden brown. Remove from the oven and let cool on the baking sheets.

Make the syrup by combining the remaining 1 cup (200 grams) sugar, honey, cinnamon stick, lemon zest, and ¾ cup (175 milliliters) water in a saucepan. Bring to a boil, then lower the heat and simmer for a few minutes.

Pile all of the cookies onto one baking sheet. Submerge a few at a time into the warm syrup. Let them sit in the syrup for about a minute, then remove with a slotted spoon to the empty baking sheet. Continue to soak the remaining cookies in batches.

Once all the cookies are soaked with syrup, sprinkle with the ground walnuts. Arrange on a serving platter in a beautiful mound.

Christmas Chocolate Log

Even if it was never the star of the show, I couldn't create a true representation of Christmas in my family without a chocolate log.   serves · 6 to 8   time · Under 3 hours

5 large eggs, separated

1½ cups plus 6 tablespoons (375 grams) granulated sugar

½ cup (50 grams) almonds, ground

½ cup (40 grams) unsweetened cocoa powder

⅓ cup (50 grams) cornstarch

1 recipe Chocolate Mousse (page 173)

4 cups (1 liter) heavy cream

Preheat the oven to 400°F (200°C). Line a 15½-by-10½-inch (40-by-30-centimeter) jelly roll pan with parchment paper.

Beat the egg whites with 3 tablespoons of the sugar to form stiff peaks. Beat the yolks with 3 tablespoons of the sugar until pale and thick.

Combine the ground almonds, cocoa powder, and cornstarch and add to the yolks in three parts, alternating with the egg whites. Mix together gently until just combined.

Pour the batter into the jelly roll pan and smooth out with a spatula or the back of a spoon.

Bake in the oven for 12 to 15 minutes. Remove from the oven and immediately invert onto a tea towel. Pull the parchment paper off carefully and then roll the cake up in the towel to keep it moist. Let the cake cool.

Combine the remaining 1½ cups (300 grams) sugar and 1¼ cups (300 milliliters) water in a saucepan and place over medium heat. Bring to a boil, then reduce the heat and simmer for 10 minutes. Remove from the heat and let cool.

Make the chocolate mousse as instructed on page 173. Whip the cream and combine the mousse with half of the whipped cream. Reserve the remaining whipped cream for serving.

Once cool, unroll the cake. Drizzle the syrup evenly over the cake with a ladle, then evenly spread with the chocolate mousse filling. With the aid of the tea towel, roll up the cake again, working gently so that the filling doesn't ooze out of the sides. Transfer to a serving platter and decorate with the reserved whipped cream just before serving.

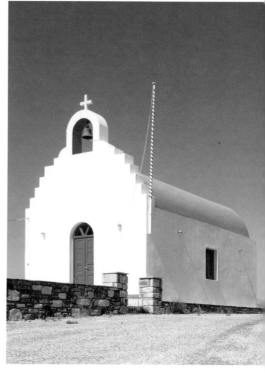

Chestnut Pavlova

We make this dessert for Christmas lunch in my home because my mother loves it. To me, chestnuts epitomize the magic of autumn and winter and must not be consumed outside of their season, however much we crave them. They do not need our help to be glorious; they are intrinsically subtle but composite in flavor.

serves • 10 to 12   time • Under 3 hours

1 cup plus 2 tablespoons (225 grams) granulated sugar

3 large egg whites

2½ pounds (1.2 kilograms) shell-on chestnuts or two (14.8-ounce / 420-gram) jars peeled and roasted chestnuts

2 cups (500 milliliters) milk, plus more as needed for consistency

1 tablespoon unsweetened cocoa powder

1 tablespoon vanilla extract

2 cups (500 milliliters) heavy cream

Preheat the oven to 275°F (135°C). Line a baking sheet with parchment paper.

Measure out 3 tablespoons of the sugar and set aside to make the chestnut mixture.

With an electric mixer, beat the egg whites until they form soft peaks, then beat in the remaining sugar a tablespoon at a time. The meringue is ready when it has a smooth but firm texture. When you tip the bowl upside down, the meringue should not fall. Spoon it onto the lined baking sheet in a round shape and level with a spatula.

Bake in the oven for 1 hour. Turn off the oven and let it sit in the oven for 30 minutes more. Once the meringue is dry and completely cool, put it on a round platter.

Meanwhile, prepare the whole chestnuts, if using. Make a slit in the shell of each chestnut starting on the thick end and going down. Bring a large pot of water to a boil, add the chestnuts, and boil for 25 minutes. Remove the pot from the heat and let the chestnuts cool in the water. Once cool enough to handle, use a small knife to peel off the thick outer shell.

Discard the water in the pot and add the peeled or jarred chestnuts back to the pot along with the milk. Bring to a boil over medium heat, and cook until they are just soft enough to mash with a wooden spoon. Add the remaining 3 tablespoons sugar, the cocoa, and vanilla, and cook until the mixture thickens. Add more milk if the chestnuts have absorbed it all. Remove from the heat and let cool.

Whip the cream and place it in a pastry bag with a decorative tip. Chill in the fridge for 30 minutes.

To assemble the pavlova: Pack the chestnut mixture into a potato ricer and press some through, letting it fall directly onto the meringue base, then pipe some whipped cream on top. Continue to layer chestnut mixture and whipped cream, forming a cone-like mound and ending with the chestnut mixture.

Decorate the edges with whipped cream, using your imagination.

Roast Suckling Pig

My father always cooked, though he rarely used recipes, and his specialties were dishes that he could make in very little time. He has a particularly refined taste, but did not put himself to the test of re-creating the dishes that he loves until I returned from cooking school and became his easy source of cooking knowledge. Recently, he has started to cook elaborate meals for his friends and family, and I must say, he is an excellent cook! The past few years, we have celebrated New Year's Eve or Christmas Eve with Daddy's large roast suckling pig. This recipe is laborious and requires a watchful eye the whole time. To my thinking, there is something primitive about roasting a whole animal. It transports me back to a time when feasts were times of great celebration, and everyday meals were modest and simple.   serves • 12 to 14   time • Under 8 hours

Salt and pepper

One (13- to 18-pound / 6- to 8-kilogram) suckling pig

tip

If you want to make this roast for fewer people, buy half a suckling pig and treat it in the same way. The roasting time will be shorter, but all else will remain the same.

Preheat the oven to 320°F (160°C).

Mix together a generous amount of salt and pepper in a bowl, about one part pepper to three parts salt. Season each leg by making a small hole on the inside part of the joint and filling it with salt and pepper with your finger. Do this for all four joints. Then rub the whole pig with salt and pepper inside and out.

Place the pig on an oven rack facedown with its legs spread out. If it does not fit in your oven, do not worry, just turn the pig on its side. Place a rack in the middle of the oven and put a baking pan underneath it on another rack; fill the pan with water to keep the meat moist (you will need to add water throughout the cooking process).

Roast the pig in the oven for 6 to 8 hours, allowing 1 hour for every 2 pounds (1 kilogram). After 2 hours, increase the temperature to 350°F (180°C). If you see that the skin starts to get dark early on, cover it loosely with a piece of foil. For the final 45 minutes of roasting, increase the temperature to 400°F (200°C) and remove the foil so that the skin becomes crispy.

Pierce the meat every so often while roasting. The meat is ready when it is so soft it melts in your mouth.

Remove the pig from the oven and set on a large cutting board. Let it rest for 10 minutes before carving. To serve, start by cutting small succulent pieces of crunchy skin and meat off the roast for your guests to eat with their fingers as they stand around waiting for the feast to begin. Then cut the roast into pieces and serve on a platter.

All Things Good

Do not share a recipe you love
Omit an ingredient when giving a recipe
Don't share what you eat
Eat too much
Compete to be the best cook
Tell someone that his or her food is disgusting
Become possessive
Snatch a biscuit out of someone's hand
Do not feed someone who is hungry
Put someone's mouth on fire by adding too much
chili to your food
Serve yourself the last portion at the table without
wondering if anyone else wants it
Never make homemade meals
Eat junk food all the time
Forget about where and how what you eat is grown
Do not be in touch with the seasons or nature
Always eat alone while watching television
Travel to another country and don't eat the
local food
Do not try anything new
Eat the same thing every day
Throw leftovers away
And live in a world with no hope

or

choose to live something different

Essential Recipes

At cooking school, I acquired a solid foundation that I can use whenever I want to create something in the kitchen. In this chapter, I pay tribute to this valuable knowledge and give you the essential recipes that underlie Greek cuisine. As you will see, many of them appear as the base of other recipes in this cookbook.

Once you have tried a few recipes from this book, I hope that you will start to make personal alterations based on things that you have learned.

Hopefully, through the use of this book, you will acquire a little more confidence when it comes to kitchen matters. I encourage you to move beyond what you have already mastered and the past you have known to venture into the unknown.

Stocks

Here are a few important things to know when you make stock:

- How long it takes to make stock will depend on the amount of vegetables, chicken, or meat you use relative to the volume of water. If you want your stock to be concentrated and take less time to cook, use a larger quantity of ingredients with a smaller amount of water than specified in the recipe.

- The more you reduce a stock the more concentrated the flavor.

- Do not salt stock; keep it basic and salt the food you are enhancing with the stock.

- You can use vegetable scraps to make stock; you do not need the whole vegetable.

- Even if you are increasing the amount of water in your stock, do not add more celery. Celery adds a complex undertone to stock, but if used in excess can overpower any other flavor.

- If you want to make extra stock to freeze and have handy, double the recipe. Freeze for up to 1 month in an ice cube tray (this will allow you to use smaller portions of it at one time, if desired, and defrost it quickly), or in a glass container so that it will not take on any unwanted flavors.

Vegetable Stock

Vegetable stock can be made from the peelings and trimmings of vegetables—just put all this "waste" in a plastic bag and keep it in the freezer until you have a small bagful. If you don't have any leftover vegetable trimmings, follow the recipe below. You can use this recipe as a substitute for water or beef or chicken stock in any recipe; it takes less time and requires less preparation than the other stocks.   makes • 1 to 1¹/₂ quarts (1 to 1.5 liters)

1 carrot, coarsely chopped

1 leek, green part only,
  coarsely chopped

1 onion, coarsely chopped

1 tomato, coarsely chopped

4 to 5 sprigs parsley

5 to 10 black peppercorns

1 sprig thyme or rosemary

1 clove garlic

1 whole clove

Combine all ingredients in an 8-quart (7.5-liter) stockpot and cover with water (about 8 cups / 2 liters). Bring to a boil, then reduce the heat and simmer for about 1 hour. Strain and use immediately, refrigerate for up to 5 days, or freeze for up to 1 month.

tip

If you want to convert this stock into a wonderful velouté soup, use whole vegetables and fill the pot up with water to cover the vegetables comfortably. After cooking, remove the clove and peppercorns and, using a food processor or a handheld blender, blend it and season with salt and pepper.

Chicken Stock

Convert this chicken stock into a chicken soup whenever you are in need of a warm hug, a good dose of nutrition, or something to show you that everything is going to be all right. To do this, use a whole free-range chicken instead of bones and add half the amount of water. Once you have finished cooking it, let the chicken cool and remove all the meat from the bone with your hands. Put the meat back into the broth, reheat, and eat.   makes · 2 to 2¹/₂ quarts (2 to 2.5 liters)

Extra-virgin olive oil

1¹/₂ pounds (700 grams) chicken bones, or 1 whole free-range chicken

1 onion, coarsely chopped

1 carrot, coarsely chopped

1 leek, green part only, coarsely chopped

1 tomato, coarsely chopped

1 stalk celery, coarsely chopped

4 to 5 sprigs parsley

5 to 10 black peppercorns

1 sprig thyme or rosemary

1 bay leaf

1 whole clove

If using the whole chicken, wash and pat dry. Add a drizzle of oil to an 8-quart (7.5-liter) stockpot over high heat. Add all the ingredients and stir to coat with the oil. Once they've taken on some color, fill with cold water to cover (about 4 quarts / 4 liters). Bring to a boil, then reduce the heat and let simmer for as little as 30 minutes and up to 2 hours.

Keep a bowl of water and a slotted spoon to the side of your pot to skim off any foam that rises to the top while cooking.

Strain and use immediately, refrigerate for up to 3 days, or freeze for up to 1 month.

If you use a whole chicken to make the stock, use the chicken meat to make a chicken salad.

Beef Stock

Beef stock is no different from other stocks in that it adds flavor to any sauce or stew it is used in. But when compared to chicken stock, for example, it has a much heavier flavor and has much more presence in your finished dish than any other stock. When reduced to about one-tenth its original volume, it becomes a potent meat sauce in itself.   makes • 2 to 2½ quarts (2 to 2.5 liters)

Extra-virgin olive oil

1 to 1½ pounds (500 to 700 grams) beef bones, cut in small pieces (the more the merrier), or ¾ pound (350 grams) oxtail

1 carrot, coarsely chopped

1 onion, coarsely chopped

1 leek, green part only, coarsely chopped

4 to 5 sprigs parsley

1 sprig thyme or rosemary

1 bay leaf

10 black peppercorns

1 cup (250 milliliters) red wine

6 tablespoons tomato paste

To use the same day, use the same amount of ingredients in a much smaller amount of water and boil for 1 hour.

The more marrow your bones have, the more gelatinous your final stock will be—which will give your sauces a thicker and smoother consistency.

Add a generous drizzle of oil to an 8-quart (7.5-liter) stockpot over high heat. When nearly smoking, add the bones. Let them stick to the bottom of the pan—be calculatedly careless. Cook them until nearly charred.

Add the vegetables, herbs, and spices and cook them until they take on some color. Let the situation get out of hand. Add the red wine and reduce until there is absolutely no liquid left. Add the tomato paste and let it stick to the pan. Just when you think it may burn, add cold water to fill the pot nearly to the brim (about 4 quarts / 4 liters).

Boil over medium heat for 2 hours without a lid, until it reduces to half the volume. Keep a small bowl of water with a slotted spoon on the side to remove the foam as it rises to the top.

Once ready, strain and let cool completely. Chill in a container with a lid overnight and scrape off the layer of fat that has collected on top the next morning. Refrigerate for up to 3 days or freeze for up to 1 month.

Tomato Sauce

This recipe is the base for many of the dishes in the book, but can also be used on its own as a simple pasta sauce. Buy a large amount of aromatic ripe tomatoes in the summer, make as much sauce as you please, and store in jars to have throughout the barren winter months.   makes • 2 cups (500 milliliters)

Extra-virgin olive oil

1 onion, finely chopped

1 clove garlic, crushed

Salt and pepper

6 fresh tomatoes, grated, or one 14-ounce (400-gram) can diced tomatoes

1 bay leaf

1 teaspoon sugar

Coat a deep frying pan with olive oil and place over medium heat. Add the onion and garlic and a pinch of salt. Stir to coat the onion in the oil, then add a dash of water. Cook until the onion is soft, translucent, and is starting to take on some color.

Add the tomatoes and let them boil vigorously for 5 minutes, making sure they don't get stuck to the bottom of the pan. Add 1 cup (250 milliliters) water and the bay leaf and sugar and simmer over medium heat until the sauce thickens and most of the liquid has evaporated, about 20 minutes. Adjust the seasoning, adding more salt and pepper to taste. If it still tastes acidic, add a little more water and simmer for about 10 minutes more.

Mayonnaise

Mayonnaise is often thought of as difficult to make, but follow the recipe below and you will have excellent results. Due to the raw egg, mayonnaise goes bad rather quickly, so make it just before you want to use it, and throw out leftovers after two days.   <u>makes</u> • 2½ cups (600 grams)

1 large egg plus 1 egg yolk

1 tablespoon red wine vinegar

2 teaspoons Dijon mustard

¾ teaspoon salt

1½ cups (350 milliliters) sunflower oil

¾ cup (180 milliliters) extra-virgin olive oil

Pepper (optional)

Combine the whole egg and the yolk in a large mixing bowl, the bowl of your food processor, or a blender. Add the vinegar, mustard, and salt and mix.

Combine the oils and start adding them to the egg mixture in a slow and steady stream while mixing. The mayonnaise should start thickening as it incorporates the oil. Stop adding oil if you see that the mixture needs some time to absorb it. Generally, mayonnaise can absorb large amounts of oil, though if it reaches saturation it will separate (see tip).

Once you've stopped adding oil, taste the mayonnaise and adjust the salt. Season with pepper, if desired, but keep in mind that you'll see the black specks of pepper in your mayonnaise.

tip

If the mayonnaise separates, do not throw the whole thing away. Break another egg into a separate bowl, add two tablespoons of the separated mayonnaise, and beat; once combined, slowly add the rest of the mayonnaise.

Avgolemono

This sauce is a staple in Greek cuisine; we use it in various ways to enhance stews and soups, and to make a sauce thicker and smoother. The important things to remember when making avgolemono are to add the hot liquid to the egg slowly, and to keep the pot on low heat when you pour the mixture back into your dish so that it doesn't curdle. Add as much lemon as you want at the end, tasting every so often to make sure it is not too sour.   makes • 3 cups (700 milliliters)

1 large egg plus 2 egg yolks

1 tablespoon cornstarch

Juice of 1 lemon

3 cups (700 milliliters) hot cooking liquid

tip

This recipe will thicken 3 cups (700 milliliters) of liquid. Increase the ingredients proportionally according to the amount of liquid in your recipe.

Beat the whole egg, yolks, and cornstarch together with an electric mixer in a large mixing bowl. Beat until pale and fluffy. While beating, add half of the lemon juice. Once the lemon is incorporated, continue beating and start adding the hot cooking liquid, a ladleful at a time.

Once doubled in volume, pour the avgolemono into the pot containing the remaining hot cooking liquid. Place over low heat. Once you see the first bubbles start to appear, start shaking the pot over the heat for 5 minutes without letting it boil. (Keep the pot moving to prevent curdling.) Adjust the lemon juice to taste (the lemon must be present but must not overtake the other flavors), and then immediately remove the pot from the heat. Serve hot!

Béchamel

Béchamel sauce has become a terrorizing monster in myths surrounding the kitchen. I wish to dissipate the fear and even make you enjoy the process of making a béchamel. The recipe you will find here is thicker than a normal béchamel, as it is meant to be used as a coating in recipes like Pastitsio (page 39) and Moussaka (page 66). When it is used inside a dish, the recipe will call for more milk or cream.

    Once you feel sufficiently confident in this recipe, start playing with the ratio of butter to flour to achieve different textures, use oil instead of the butter for a different taste, or use one of the stocks instead of the milk to make a different type of sauce for meat or fish.   makes • 3 cups (700 milliliters)

7 tablespoons (100 grams) unsalted butter

¾ cup (100 grams) all-purpose flour

2 cups (500 milliliters) milk

3 tablespoons heavy cream

Salt and pepper

Ground nutmeg

tip

You can thin your béchamel by adding some milk or cream when you have taken it off the heat.

Melt the butter in a medium saucepan over medium heat. Add the flour all at once and stir with a wooden spoon until all the butter is absorbed.

    Add the milk, little by little, whisking constantly. The mixture should start to thicken immediately. Once all the milk is incorporated, whisk in the cream and simmer gently for 20 minutes, whisking frequently so it won't stick to the bottom of the pan. If you taste the sauce at the beginning of cooking, you will notice that the flour is raw. Keep tasting throughout and remove from the heat when you can no longer taste the raw flour.

    Season to taste with salt, pepper, and nutmeg.

Kimas
MEAT SAUCE

This meat sauce is used in several recipes in this book; once you have mastered it, you will be halfway to mastering those recipes, too. One word to remember and repeat when making this recipe is "reduction." Reduce the water from the ground meat, reduce the wine completely, reduce the tomato for less acidity—but make sure it is moist enough to keep the rest of the recipe juicy. Use this wonderful sauce as is for a delicious accompaniment to pasta.   makes • 4 cups (1 liter)

Extra-virgin olive oil

1 large onion, finely chopped

Salt and pepper

1⅓ pounds (600 grams) ground beef

½ cup (125 milliliters) white wine

6 medium tomatoes, grated, or one 14-ounce (400-gram) can diced tomatoes

1½ teaspoons sugar, or to taste

1 bay leaf

2 allspice berries

½ teaspoon ground cinnamon

Pinch ground cloves

3 cups (750 milliliters) Vegetable Stock (page 210) or Beef Stock (page 212)

In a large frying pan over medium heat, add enough olive oil to just cover the bottom. Add the onion and cook gently, letting it caramelize. Add a pinch of salt to help the onion cook in its juices.

Add the beef and increase the heat to medium high. Brown the meat, stirring well to break it apart. Once browned, add the wine and boil vigorously until all the alcohol has evaporated.

Add the tomatoes, lower heat to medium, and simmer until slightly thickened. Add the sugar, bay leaf, allspice, cinnamon, cloves, and stock. Season with salt and pepper. Let simmer for 30 to 35 minutes, until most of the water has evaporated. The sauce should be thick, but not too dry.

Season with salt and pepper to taste. If you find the sauce to be too acidic, add a teaspoon of sugar and simmer for 10 to 15 minutes longer. Pluck out the bay leaf and allspice berries before serving.

Reduce the wine completely to ensure minimum acidity. At first, you will notice the smell of alcohol, but as the mixture simmers the alcohol will continue to evaporate. By the time the sauce is fully cooked, you want to be inhaling just the aroma of the wine, without the alcohol.

Savory Pastry Case

Like a pizza crust, a savory pastry case can be filled with just about anything. You can use the Onion Tart on page 105 as inspiration, substituting the onions with another vegetable you love, or swapping the Gruyère or Parmesan for a different cheese.

makes • Enough dough for one 10- to 12-inch (25- to 30-centimeter) tart pan

2 cups (250 grams) all-purpose flour, plus more for pan

Pinch salt

3/4 cup (1½ sticks / 170 grams) unsalted butter, cut into small pieces, plus more for greasing

2/3 cup (50 grams) grated Parmesan or a cheese of your choice

1 large egg

Put the flour and salt in a large bowl. Add the butter and combine the ingredients by gently rubbing between both hands, until the mixture looks like coarse breadcrumbs.

Add the cheese, the egg, and 1 tablespoon water and continue kneading with your hands. If the dough still doesn't come together, add an additional tablespoon water. Work together, handling as little as possible, until it is a smooth dough. Wrap in parchment paper and chill in the fridge for at least 20 minutes or up to 2 days. (You'll need to take the dough out of the fridge 20 minutes before you intend to use it if it has sat in the fridge for a long time.)

If you wish to blind bake the crust: Preheat the oven to 350°F (180°C). Grease a loose-bottomed tart pan by rubbing with a piece of butter. Add a handful of flour. Move the pan around to spread the flour everywhere. Turn the pan over and bang it down on your work surface to remove the excess flour.

Unwrap the dough, knead it a little, then use a rolling pin to roll it into a round a bit larger than the diameter of your tart pan. Transfer to your prepared tart pan. Trim away excess pastry, but ensure a little extra is left at the sides of the pan, as the pastry shrinks as it bakes. Prick the bottom all over with a fork, cover with foil and fill with pie weights or dried beans, and bake in the oven for 25 minutes. Remove the foil and pie weights and bake an additional 10 minutes, until the pastry is golden and set.

Sweet Pastry Case

Here is a crumbly pastry recipe you can use as the base for any dessert, be it Pasta Flora with homemade jam (page 74), lemon tart, or baked fruit pie, to name a few.   <u>makes</u> • Enough dough for one 10- to 12-inch (25- to 30-centimeter) tart pan

2 cups (250 grams) all-purpose flour, plus more for pan

⅓ cup (80 grams) turbinado sugar

Pinch salt

Zest of 1 lemon

¾ cup (1½ sticks / 170 grams) unsalted butter, plus more for greasing

1 large egg yolk

1 teaspoon vanilla extract

1 tablespoon milk

1 tablespoon brandy or Cognac (optional)

Combine the flour, sugar, salt, and zest in a large bowl. Cut the butter into small pieces over the bowl. Gently rub the ingredients between both hands, until the mixture looks like coarse breadcrumbs.

Add the egg yolk, vanilla, milk, and brandy, if using. Work until the dough starts coming together, handling as little as possible. Add 1 tablespoon of water if the dough is still dry. Wrap in parchment paper and chill in the fridge for at least 20 minutes or up to 2 days. (You'll need to take the dough out of the fridge 20 minutes before you intend to use it if it has sat in the fridge for a long time.)

If you wish to blind bake the crust (for a fruit tart or or lemon pie, for example): Preheat the oven to 375°F (190°C). Grease a loose-bottomed tart pan by rubbing with a piece of butter. Add a handful of flour. Move the pan around to spread the flour everywhere. Turn the pan over and bang it down on your work surface to remove the excess flour.

Unwrap the dough, knead it a little, then use a rolling pin to roll it into a round a bit larger than the diameter of your tart pan. Transfer the pastry to the tart pan. Trim away excess pastry, but ensure a little extra is left at the sides of the pan, as the pastry shrinks as it bakes.

Prick the bottom all over with a fork, cover with foil and pie weights or dried beans, and bake in the oven for 25 minutes. Remove the foil and pie weights and bake an additional 10 minutes, until the pastry is golden and set.

Leaps of Faith

I agree with those who say that creation requires a leap of faith.

But if there is no place to leap off, there is no leap and there is no creation.

Well, there may be creation but no point of reference to know that where you land is different from where you started.

For all you know, you could be leaping up and down in the same place, which could be comforting, because you always land back where you were without knowing where that exactly is.

Which totally obliterates the idea of starting from somewhere and going somewhere else, which is the thing that required the leap in the first place.

And what about faith? Why are you making a leap of faith?
Well, because if we presuppose that you now know where you are starting from, you definitely don't know exactly what you are going to meet when you land. There is a flexible trajectory that could be intercepted by just about anything.

So all in all, it seems like a scary thing to make a leap of faith.
So we just stay put, not knowing where we started, never wanting to find out— because anyway we don't really want to leave it.

Or do we?

To Kyria Loula

YOUR NAME WAS SPIRIDOULA, but they called you Loula. You cooked food for three generations of the same family and saw everything from the outside in. One Monday night, you closed your eyes and flew, light like a feather in the wind, never to return but always to be remembered through the recipes in this book.

Without you, your recipes seem like bare bones of a building with nothing to fill the spaces of your absence. You spoke the life into them: the smells, the tastes, and the process. They were full when with you.

You were not a big woman in size, and as the years went by you became slighter by the day, but you had the heart and strength of a glorious fighter. You liked to complain that nobody loved you, that life had dealt you bad cards, and it was true: life hadn't taken much care to give your story many happy turns. But despite this, you had a huge capacity to give and care for others, and a certain optimism when it came to other people's lives. It seems deep down you knew that without hardship, life was like one of those empty recipes that begs to be given some soul.

You were intuitive and knew exactly what was going on in the kitchen and out. You created just enough drama to keep things exciting. You liked to gossip or talk to people on the phone for ages to keep you company and alleviate the loneliness you may have felt inside. You provoked some teasing from the younger members of the families you cooked for, but reveled in their attention and loved it when their young arms gave you hugs and massaged your pain-ridden body.

You were not brought up to be refined, but you had your own sense of sophistication. You wished to find new recipes, to become better, to be praised for the delicious meals you prepared, and through this you created a pillar to support yourself when all else had crumbled and kept crumbling around you.

You took your time to perfect your food, and it was this secret ingredient that made the recipes you cooked so special, even if it was often misunderstood. There were times you got carried away and altered your dishes according to your whim, which slightly aggravated those looking for that familiar and delicious taste of your food.

You believed in God just the way the Orthodox Church commanded and felt sad for those who didn't have the same respect for religion, yet it was not in your nature to try to convert those with other interpretations of the mystery of life. Even though you seemed conservative, you were modern in a timeless way, a quality that gave you the ability to understand things that, perhaps, one would assume you would not have understood.

You let things get stuck to the bottom of the pan so that you could scrape it and make your food tastier. You drank coffee in a strange way and drank ice-cold water whether it was summer or winter. You never made fresh phyllo pastry or bread, shying away from this for fear of failure. Your cakes never came out the same way twice, but you were fantastic at making any type of cookie, savory or sweet. You liked eating other people's food more than your own, and did not cook with the same pleasure for yourself as you did for others.

You encouraged, you reassured, and hearing those words from you, who had lived through so much, meant the world.

To Giagia Sofia

YOU WERE NOT THERE ON THAT DAY. The family was gathered in the warmth of your house, which was far from warm with you not there. Your role had always been to bring them close when they were far apart, and this occasion was no different.

The family's Sunday lunch gatherings required a certain amount of preparation; preparation they knew gave you much pleasure and pride. You protected the kitchen with shouts of concealed love from the influx of grandchildren, who were curious to discover the glory of your food and the long-forgotten chocolates in the chocolate drawer.

You were always as present as your criticism, which at times was well received, and at other times caused an escalation of familiar voices to fill the dining room. It always surprised them when you held back from demonstrating your love with such discipline in those times. You looked at them with revealing eyes, your wrinkles presaging the myriad expressions you made in response to anything anyone said. Your skin was like a beautiful material one just has to touch.

In the past you would tease the "silly" grandchildren for turning up at your house in jeans and then-fashionable yellow hiking boots, especially the girls. You believed that Sunday lunch should be a well-respected ritual, and that it definitely merited a skirt. But fashion got ahold of you, and there came a time when you started wearing the jeans you so looked down upon and the pointy shoes you often criticized others for wearing. It seems that things do change. People change. You changed, too. Your immense softness, long buried under the cloaks of your past and your strong-headed appearance, started to fade, and the grandchildren really appreciated that. They told you that they loved you sometimes, and you would respond with a laugh and a flick of the head. You acted like you didn't much like sentimentality, but they knew that you secretly loved it. After all, it was you who had taught them that they should follow their hearts. They were always listening attentively to your words, even if they didn't always show it. Around you, it was not the words and actions in themselves that mattered, but the intentions behind them.

You took your five grandchildren out to dinner often. The pride you felt for each and every one of them was stifled as they surrounded you at the table. You demonstrated your love through your refined art of poking where it really hurts.

The last time you sat across from your granddaughter, you listened to her thoughts on life and dreams and love with unusual excitement, your beautiful, wrinkle-filled face beaming at hers in adoration. It was obvious neither you nor she knew it would be the last time. You urged her on.

You were a distinguished person then and now, even when you are no longer here.

End Note

THIS BOOK HAS BEEN ON QUITE A JOURNEY before landing in your hands. It started as *Cooking to Share*, a Kickstarter project with 543 people anticipating its release. It has had two design teams, one photographer, two printers, two text editors, and two recipe editors.

The first version was printed by Alta Grafico—who did an incredible job at rendering the design into a beautiful book to hold, designed by G Design Studio, who found the most elegant way of translating the warmth I wished to capture and the usability that I find necessary in a cookbook. It was photographed by Ioanna Roufopoulou, who sat patiently over the food to be shot and waited until I thought it told a real-enough story. It then gained two fairy godmothers, Chris Wren and Katie Capaldi. Chris showed *Cooking to Share* to Katie, an owner of a bookshop called Between the Covers in Harbor Springs, Michigan (a place I didn't even know), and Katie showed it to Artisan. Then Artisan came into the picture, applied its experience and expertise, and made *Cooking with Loula* what you see it to be.

This book is a testament to my voyage through my past, but also a reminder to myself of the things I believe to be important: our connection to the land, the people we care for, and the basic sustenance of our existence. The last time I wrote an end note for this book, I felt an overwhelming surge of movement and a feeling of wholly rooted independence; both of which then made me slightly uncomfortable. I think it is safe to say that I am now well on my way to creating new paths and feel tremendous gratitude to all the people who have joined and continue to join me in my adventures.

Thank you for the continued support, the conversations, the encouragement, the belief, and the positivity. I wish not to name each and every one of you because my gratitude extends in the same measure to everyone: the people who have employed their skills to help create this book in its first and second phases; the people I may have exchanged one email with; and those who have been by my side while making this book into what you see today.

I especially wish to thank those first 543 people who bought a book that wasn't even made yet, over the Internet, from a stranger—without them, this book would never have come into being.

Recipe List

by Time and Course

RECIPE	PAGE	TIME	COURSE
Tyrokafteri (Spicy Cheese Dip)	138	Under 30 min.	Meze
Taramosalata (Cod Roe Dip)	152	Under 30 min.	Meze
Skordalia (Garlic Dip)	183	Under 30 min.	Meze
Green Salad with Red Cabbage and Fruits	48	Under 30 min.	Salad
Lahano Karoto (Cabbage and Carrot Salad)	61	Under 30 min.	Salad
A Simple Green Salad	94	Under 30 min.	Salad
Greek Salad	135	Under 30 min.	Salad
Vrasta Lahanika (Boiled Vegetables)	168	Under 30 min.	Salad
Strapatsada (Scrambled Eggs with Tomato Sauce)	47	Under 30 min.	Main
Cheese and Ham on Toast, Topped with a Fried Egg	72	Under 30 min.	Main
Fried Vegetables	156	Under 1 hr.	Meze
Fried Squid	157	Under 1 hr.	Meze
Traganisti Araviki Pita (Pita Bread Crisps)	158	Under 1 hr.	Meze
Kaiki Tuna Salad	130	Under 1 hr.	Salad
Lavraki Plaki (Oven-Baked Sea Bass)	63	Under 1 hr.	Main
Arakas (Oil-Stewed Green Peas)	64	Under 1 hr.	Main
Spinach Purée	115	Under 1 hr.	Side
Potato Purée	116	Under 1 hr.	Side
Carrot Purée	117	Under 1 hr.	Side
Semolina Halva	76	Under 1 hr.	Dessert
Cooked Uncooked Chocolate Cake	125	Under 1 hr.	Dessert
Svigous (Fried Dough Balls with Syrup)	169	Under 1 hr.	Dessert
Tyropitakia (Mini Cheese Pies)	133	Under 2 hr.	Meze
Fava (Yellow Split Pea Purée)	142	Under 2 hr.	Meze
Melitzanosalata (Roasted Eggplant Dip)	148	Under 2 hr.	Meze
Keftedakia (Mini Meatballs)	151	Under 2 hr.	Meze
Salata me Mavromatika (Black-Eyed Pea Salad)	132	Under 2 hr.	Salad
Charlotte's Potato Salad	164	Under 2 hr.	Salad
Fakes (Lentil Soup)	50	Under 2 hr.	Soup
Butternut Squash Soup	122	Under 2 hr.	Soup
Soutzoukakia (Spiced Meatballs in Tomato Sauce)	32	Under 2 hr.	Main
Spanakopita (Spinach Pie)	34	Under 2 hr.	Main
Gemista (Stuffed Tomatoes and Peppers)	36	Under 2 hr.	Main
Kokkinisto Kotopoulo (Tomato-Stewed Chicken with Orzo)	40	Under 2 hr.	Main
Briam (Oven-Baked Vegetables)	44	Under 2 hr.	Main
Chicken Milaneza	59	Under 2 hr.	Main
Kotopoulo sto Fourno (Chicken in the Oven)	70	Under 2 hr.	Main
Kotopoulo Lemonato (Lemon Chicken Stew)	89	Under 2 hr.	Main
Fasolakia me Garides (Green Beans and Shrimp)	102	Under 2 hr.	Main
Pasta au Gratin	106	Under 2 hr.	Main
Artichokes à la Polita	108	Under 2 hr.	Main
Pork Tenderloin in Mustard Sauce	114	Under 2 hr.	Main
Spinach Gnocchi	118	Under 2 hr.	Main
Kolokithopita (Zucchini Pie)	167	Under 2 hr.	Main

RECIPE	PAGE	TIME	COURSE
Bakaliaros Tiganitos (Deep-Fried Salt Cod)	180	Under 2 hr.	Main
Accordion Potatoes	90	Under 2 hr.	Side
Christmas Stuffing	195	Under 2 hr.	Side
Pasta Flora (Jam Tart)	74	Under 2 hr.	Dessert
Crème Caramel	77	Under 2 hr.	Dessert
Orange Cake and Marble Cake	80	Under 2 hr.	Dessert
Baklava	171	Under 2 hr.	Dessert
Vasilopita (New Year's Cake)	176	Under 2 hr.	Dessert
Layered Chocolate Birthday Cake	177	Under 2 hr.	Dessert
Koulourakia (Easter Butter Cookies)	184	Under 2 hr.	Dessert
Strawberry or Apricot Jam	190	Under 2 hr.	Jam
Octopus Marinated in Vinegar	139	Under 3 hr.	Meze
Dolmadakia (Stuffed Grape Leaves)	146	Under 3 hr.	Meze
Fasolada (White Bean Soup)	56	Under 3 hr.	Soup
Pastitsio	39	Under 3 hr.	Main
Fasolakia Ladera (Green Beans Braised in Oil)	53	Under 3 hr.	Main
Papoutsakia (Stuffed Zucchini)	54	Under 3 hr.	Main
Moussaka	66	Under 3 hr.	Main
Stuffed Crêpe Cannelloni	68	Under 3 hr.	Main
Hunkiar Beyendi (Beef Stew with Smoked Eggplant Purée)	84	Under 3 hr.	Main
Kotopita (Chicken Pie)	86	Under 3 hr.	Main
Yiouvetsi me Hilopites (Oven-Stewed Meat with Egg Pasta)	101	Under 3 hr.	Main
Onion Tart	105	Under 3 hr.	Main
Oven-Roasted Lamb	192	Under 3 hr.	Main
Pita me Lahanika (Vegetable Pie)	109	Under 3 hr.	Main
Roast Pork with Apple and Onion	112	Under 3 hr.	Main
Psito Psari (Grilled or Broiled Fish)	162	Under 3 hr.	Main
Mosaico	79	Under 3 hr.	Dessert
Apple Soufflé	123	Under 3 hr.	Dessert
Aunt Eleni's Galaktoboureko	126	Under 3 hr.	Dessert
Chocolate Mousse	173	Under 3 hr.	Dessert
Kourabiethes	197	Under 3 hr.	Dessert
Melomakarona	198	Under 3 hr.	Dessert
Christmas Chocolate Log	199	Under 3 hr.	Dessert
Chestnut Pavlova	202	Under 3 hr.	Dessert
Revithada (Oven-Baked Chickpea Soup)	188	Under 4 hr.	Main
Melitzanes Laderes (Oven-Baked Eggplant)	160	Under 4 hr.	Side
Tsoureki (Easter Bread)	186	Under 4 hr.	Bread
Lahanodolmades (Stuffed Cabbage Leaves)	92	4 hr. or longer	Main
Pork with Celeriac	95	4 hr. or longer	Main
Beef Stifado	99	4 hr. or longer	Main
Gavros Marinatos	143	Under 8 hr.	Meze
Roast Suckling Pig	204	Under 8 hr.	Main

Index

Page numbers in *italics* refer to illustrations.